Her Ladyship's

GUIDE TO THE
BRITISH SEASON

Her Ladyship's

GUIDE TO THE
BRITISH SEASON

CAROLINE TAGGART

National Trust

Author's note: some of the events in this book take place over several months (Glyndebourne) or do not reliably occur in the same month each year (the Lord's Test). In creating chapters, I have allocated such events to the month in which they usually begin or in which they often fall. It's not an exact science, so please feel free to use the index to find the event you are looking for.

First published in the United Kingdom in 2013 by
National Trust Books
10 Southcombe Street
London W14 0RA

An imprint of Anova Books Company Ltd

ISBN 9781907892288

A CIP catalogue record for this book is available from the British Library.

21 20 19 18 17 16 15 14 13
10 9 8 7 6 5 4 3 2 1

Reproduction by Mission Productions Ltd, Hong Kong
Printed and bound by Everbest Printing Ltd, China

This book can be ordered direct from the publisher at the website www.anovabooks.com, or try your local bookshop. Also available at National Trust shops and shop.nationaltrust.org.uk.

ACKNOWLEDGEMENTS

Even Her Ladyship doesn't know everything about everything, much as she would like to pretend she does. I certainly don't and am always grateful to friends who allow me to pick their brains. Special thanks this time to Jill, for excellent tips on Ascot, Henley and not sitting on the ground when you don't have to; Ros, who really did wear the same hat as Princess Margaret to a Buckingham Palace garden party; Ryan, who knows more about horse racing than most people need to; Gill, for telling me about the Grand Prix; and Rebecca, always a fount of wisdom, particularly about the colour of shoes.

Thanks also to Kristy, whose idea this book was, and everyone else at Anova and the National Trust for helping me bring it to fruition.

Contents

A Scottish Interlude

Seven
July 96
The Lord's Test, British Grand Prix, Cartier International Polo,
The Open Championship

An Irish Interlude

Eight
August 118
Glorious Goodwood, Cowes Week, The Glorious Twelfth,
Burghley Horse Trials

Nine
Out of Season 132
Edinburgh Festival Fringe, Braemar Gathering,
St Leger, Last Night of the Proms, Wexford Festival,
London to Brighton Veteran Car Run, Literary Festivals,
Burns Night, Crufts

PART I

One

WHAT IS
THE SEASON?

Ah! – those wonderful parties in town, Season after Season, when we danced until dawn – those long summer afternoons, when we sauntered through the gardens of the great houses that entertained us in those days...

J B Priestley (1894–1984)

Her Ladyship will start by not beating about the bush. For many years – over 150 years, at a conservative estimate – the Season existed to give aristocratic young ladies the opportunity to ally themselves to suitable young men. Yes, girls were presented at court; yes, they went to balls and dinner dances, Royal Ascot and Goodwood; yes, they wore gorgeous dresses and partied till four in the morning, but really what they were doing was looking for husbands.

The idea of girls being presented to royalty to mark their 'coming out' into Society at the age of seventeen or eighteen was inaugurated in 1780, when George III gave a ball to celebrate the birthday of his wife, Queen Charlotte, and to raise funds for the London hospital to be founded in her name. (A descendant of that hospital still exists, and until quite recently blue-blooded women paid their respects to its royal benefactress by having their babies there.) By the early nineteenth century being presented at court was an established custom and the girls making their debut had become known as debutantes. 'Curtseying' – there was no need to specify to whom – was a part of every debutante's career until Queen Elizabeth II discontinued the practice in the increasingly egalitarian world of 1958.

Court presentations were surrounded by a code of etiquette as rigid as any whalebone corset. A girl being presented had to be sponsored by a lady, normally her mother, who had herself been presented. It was as simple and as unyielding as that. If the mother was deceased or (perish the thought) divorced, an aunt, grandmother or close friend could take her place. Such a system obviously made it very difficult for outsiders to gain access to it, and the extent to which the 'Upper Ten Thousand' of Society intermingled and intermarried only confirmed its exclusivity.

As the growth of industry and trade brought wealth to non-aristocrats, however, and inheritance tax or reckless extravagance took it away from those who had been born with it, money began to speak more loudly: a prosperous merchant's daughter could marry an impoverished peer and gain access to High Society, if not for herself then at least for her children. Call it broadening the gene pool, call it lowering the tone – either way, even in the nineteenth century, times were beginning to change.

By the twentieth century, a handful of Society matrons with an eye for the main chance supplemented their income by sponsoring the daughters of anyone who was willing to pay. This obviously brought the whole system to the brink of disrepute: as early as 1938 *Vogue* was describing 'yammering hordes of social "racketeers" [who] have introduced madness into method and turned a traditional practice into a flourishing industry'. So unexclusive had court

In the much-quoted and possibly apocryphal words of the late Princess Margaret, 'We had to put a stop to it. Every tart in London was getting in.'

presentations become by the 1950s that, in the much-quoted and possibly apocryphal words of the late Princess Margaret, 'We had to put a stop to it. Every tart in London was getting in.'

QUEEN CHARLOTTE'S BALL

The ball that started it all off is famous for featuring a parade of hand-picked girls in wedding-dress white escorting an enormous birthday cake. It was traditionally held in May (Her Majesty's birthday was the 19th), though of recent years its organisers have chosen a date in the autumn.

Her Ladyship would at this point like to quash a popular misconception regarding Queen Charlotte's Ball, by referring her readers to the unchallenged doyenne of social commentators, Betty Kenward, who wrote 'Jennifer's Diary' for *Tatler* and later *Harper's and Queen* for almost 50 years. In her memoir she describes the chosen debutantes pulling the cake 'with white satin ribbons, right up to the dance floor to where the ball's President and guest of honour stood in long evening dresses and tiaras'. The guest of honour might be a member of the Royal Family, a visiting foreign royal or the wife of a member of the British peerage. Whoever it was, 'Jennifer' observes rather austerely, 'The Maids of Honour always curtseyed to the two ladies, *never* to the cake, as I have seen written so often.'

There are those who would say that there were many absurdities about the Social Season, but Her Ladyship is happy to record that curtseying to a cake is not one of them.

The Social year

Indispensable though it was, a girl's presentation was a small part of the Social Season. Originally linked to the movements of the Royal Family and the workings of Parliament, the Social calendar followed much the same pattern for well over a hundred years. Up to and including the first half of the twentieth century, anyone who was anyone was in London in the spring and early summer, with court presentations normally taking place in May: these few months constituted the Season. Towards the end of July High Society dispersed, initially to seaside resorts such as Brighton and later to the more reliable sunshine of the south of France (see box, page 14). Those who preferred tradition to sun-worshipping went next to Scotland for the shooting season that began on the 'Glorious 12th' of August. There might follow a few weeks back in London during the autumn – the 'Little Season' – after which everyone retired to their country estates for hunting, Christmas and to await the coming of spring. To quote J B Priestley's *The Edwardians* (1972), these people may have been known as the 'idle rich', but their Social obligations certainly kept them very busy:

> *It was a dreadful nuisance, of course, but a fellow would have to go down to Cowes for the first week in August, then go up North to shoot the grouse or stalk the deer. A woman invited for a weekend at one of the great houses would have to take several large trunks, and then would have to be changing clothes – and always looking her best – half-a-dozen times a day. A free-and-easy life in theory, in practice it was more highly disciplined that the life of a recruit in the Life Guards.*

Priestley was writing as a sardonic outsider, but even those intimately involved in the Season would have had to admit that he was not far wrong.

A NOTE ON SUMMER HOLIDAYS

Fashions change in this area as they do in all other things.
There were times – again in the early-to-mid-twentieth
century – when members of Society would spend a few weeks
every summer in Biarritz, St Tropez or Monte Carlo. Now
that Society has been so much infiltrated by 'new money',
these resorts have, in Her Ladyship's opinion, become places
in which one would not choose to be seen dead. Cannes for
the film festival, perhaps; otherwise, a lesser-known Greek
island or somewhere in the Caribbean beginning with A
(there is quite a choice and the wider world has not yet
discovered all of them) would be more exclusive.

There were also times when the opulent luncheons,
teas, dinners and suppers that had been eaten every day for
months made it desirable to detox – although the word in
its modern sense had not been invented – in Baden Baden
or another of Europe's fashionable spas. Nowadays a day
at the Sanctuary in Central
London or a long weekend
at one of the many health-spa
hotels within easy distance of
the M25 should give the jaded
debutante all the relaxation
she needs. Her Ladyship, with
a lifetime of hard-earned
experience behind her, assures her readers that detoxing
is perfectly acceptable, even chic. It is when your thoughts
turn to rehab that you may have been overdoing it.

*Detoxing is perfectly
acceptable, even chic.
It is when your
thoughts turn to rehab
that you may have
been overdoing it.*

The Season itself

From March, then, to July, Society disported itself at an endless succession of balls, parties, concerts and sporting events – and there will be more detail about the sporting events later in the book. Many balls culminated in a hearty breakfast before the exhausted debutantes, their escorts and chaperones were allowed to go home to catch a few hours' sleep before the whole round began again later the same day. For debutantes it was not so much a question of 'I Could Have Danced All Night' as 'I Was Positively Obliged To'.

These debutantes formed the virginal, white- or pastel-clad core around which the whole Season revolved. Parents who didn't have a London residence often hired a house-with-ballroom for the Season; in either case they announced their arrival from the country with an advertisement in *The Times*. This subtly indicated to the initiated – and it was, of course, only the initiated who mattered – that their daughter, whose name was included in the advertisement, was available to receive invitations and would, in due course, be inviting her friends to her own 'coming out' ball.

The Season was a masterpiece of organisation for which mothers were largely responsible. Before the daughters were allowed out in public, their mothers made plans and compared notes over a series of lunches. Author Anne de Courcy, writing about the 1939 Season in her book *The Last Season* (1989), describes the near-desperation for young men among the mothers of marriageable daughters:

> *Every future hostess had her own address book full of the names of 'suitable' (that is, socially, though not necessarily morally or financially, impeccable) bachelors, which she swapped with her best friends and added to if she heard – or indeed overheard – another name. After a few weeks a definitive version of this pool of dancing*

partners and escorts would have emerged. When a man was on the List, and thus vouched for as matrimonially eligible, he was automatically asked to all the dances, whether or not he was known to the hostess.

One of the duties of these young men – the so-called 'debs' delights' – was, of course, to bring their partners home at the end of the evening. Innocent the girls may have been, but they had sufficient savoir faire to produce their own list of escorts who were considered NSIT – 'not safe in taxis'.

After the Second World War co-ordination of the schedule was greatly aided by the indefatigable 'Jennifer', who kept a list of the girls who were coming out each year and ensured that important balls and parties did not clash (though she herself frequently attended three or four in a single night).

Many of the girls who were presented at court had homes in the country and not all remained in London for the Season: in 1958 over 1,400 girls made their curtsey (an unusually large number, as it had been announced that there would be no more such occasions) but Jennifer's list included only 231 names. Many coming-out balls were therefore held in the parents' country houses. The London-based debutantes were invited to a succession of lavish weekend house parties, where thirty people sitting down to dinner was commonplace. Country girls who lived near Cowdray Park or Henley, for example, would time their ball to coincide with the polo or the Regatta, when friends and fellow debutantes would be eager to be in that part of the world. Again, Jennifer's published lists and freely given private advice were indispensable. The Marriage Mart, as it was known to the irreverent, was a well-oiled, as well as a well-heeled, machine.

The Season's events

Although court presentations have been a thing of the past
for over 50 years, the social occasions that accompanied them
continue; many of them maintain their own traditions, which
are covered later in the book. Some of the sporting events that
became integral to the Season date back to long before debutantes
were thought of. James I began racing at Newmarket in the early
seventeenth century and it was his grandson Charles II who made
this 'the Sport of Kings'. A generation later – still 70 years before
Queen Charlotte's first ball – Queen Anne instituted Royal Ascot.
The first Derby was in 1780, the first Cowes Week in 1826 and
the first Henley Regatta in 1839. And they still take place more
or less when they have always done – which is, to those not familiar
with Society's strict timetable, within a surprisingly short space of
time. The private view of the Royal Academy's Summer Exhibition,
generally in late May, was for a long time the first 'official' event of
the Season, and no member of High Society would have dreamed
of remaining in London after Goodwood in early August. As
recently as 1996, *The Times* commissioned Clement Freud to write
a series of six pieces about the Season; he was able to execute the
commission between 18th June and 18th July, having visited Royal
Ascot, the Lord's Test, Wimbledon, Henley, the British Grand
Prix and the Open (Golf) Tournament.

Her Ladyship cannot resist a slightly acid aside here. In
her memoir, 'Jennifer' refers to these renowned occasions as
'the hardy annuals'. She means, of course, 'the hardy perennials',
but she was being employed for her social acumen rather than
her horticultural knowledge.

The Season today

So what does the Season mean today? Fun, certainly: partying and dancing and attending some of the same events your great-great-grandmothers attended; drinking champagne or Pimm's and dressing in your finest. There are also opportunities to network (as Her Ladyship believes the modern term is), to improve social skills and poise, and to raise money for the many good causes that benefit from charity balls. Much of the rigorous etiquette that surrounded the early debutantes has gone, but there are still rules to be obeyed and dress codes to be followed. Because very few modern girls are brought up with these codes drilled into them from an early age, the next two chapters consider the accomplishments a young lady was once supposed to have and the clothes she was supposed to wear and draw on this information as a guide for the modern debutante. And because the Season is no longer as clearly defined as it used to be, the rest of the book is devoted to Social events that may or may not fall within the purist's definition of the term. But they are all places where the young and vivacious may go, see and be seen, have a good time and possibly – if that is the way their fancy takes them – find a husband.

A practical note

All the events described in this book have excellent websites (listed on pages 148–152), which give practical information on such subjects as schedules, buying tickets, wheelchair access and 'how to get there'. To avoid incessant repetition, this information is given in the individual entries only when Her Ladyship deems it of particular importance or interest. But she would underline the following general tips:

• Book early. Check up to a year in advance when tickets go on sale and whether or not there is some form of ballot (as there is for Wimbledon, for example, and for the Last Night of the Proms).

• If you are driving, remember that what to you is a thrilling day out may well be an annual pain in the neck for local residents. Don't park over private driveways or block other cars in and try to remember that other people may just want to go to the supermarket, get the chores done and barricade themselves into their houses until you and your companions have gone home.

• Be aware that in the more prestigious enclosures of many events described in this book, the use of mobile phones is specifically banned (and offenders may have their phones confiscated or even be asked to leave). This is not the organisers being stuffy: the sudden noises not only disturb your fellow guests, they could also upset the horses, the players or the caber-tossers. Turn your phone off and leave it off until you are back at the car park or the station.

• Be aware that some events and access to some enclosures are for members or by invitation only. Never, ever, attempt to gatecrash on these occasions: security is tight and at best you will suffer the ignominy of being escorted from the premises. Settle for the less prestigious enclosure or for attending on a less illustrious day, and make a note to extend your circle of acquaintance so that you receive an invitation next year.

Two

WHAT TO WEAR

I have heard with admiring submission the experience of the lady who declared that the sense of being perfectly well-dressed gives a feeling of inward tranquillity which religion is powerless to bestow.
Ralph Waldo Emerson (1803–82)

Once upon a time, but really not as long ago as all that, it would have been absurd for a race meeting or opera festival to advertise a dress code. No one attending – and certainly no one invited to appear in a royal box or 'premier enclosure' – would have needed to be told what to wear. Correct dress, like every other aspect of correct conduct, was instilled into a young lady's head by her mother from the moment she left the nursery. No longer: as we shall see in the next chapter, the emphasis in feminine education gradually moved away from the feminine and towards the educational, and social niceties that had once gone without saying ran a severe risk of going by the board. It is because of this general fall from grace that the organisers of Royal Ascot felt it necessary to revise their dress code for the 2012 meeting: to *remind* people of what was expected on a formal occasion.

Failing to dress appropriately for the occasion and the time of day would have been – and remains, at such events as the Henley Royal Regatta, Royal Ascot and the Royal Caledonian Ball – a social *faux pas* of the highest order. The great Duke of

Wellington himself was once refused admission to Almack's for turning up in pantaloons (trousers) rather than the formal evening attire of knee breeches demanded by that exclusive club[1].

In Victorian times, a lady of the first rank often had precious little to do, because her army of servants looked after housework, shopping and children. As a result, she had time to change her clothes at least three or four times a day. She also had an enviable wardrobe that allowed her to do so – either purchased from the top fashion houses or, if she was just a small step down from the top of the social ladder,

AN ASIDE ABOUT DRESS CODE
Whatever the occasion – and this applies to both sexes – members of the armed forces are always considered correctly attired in their Service Dress. Similarly, Her Ladyship knows of no event at which visitors from overseas are not welcome to wear the formal national dress of their country.

copied from those fashion houses by a dressmaker employed to produce something unique but stylish at a fraction of the cost.

Such a lady would dress plainly in the morning, when she was at home attending to domestic matters; after this she would don something more formal to make or receive 'morning calls'. If she was invited to or was hosting a tea party – at five o'clock, after the morning calls had been dealt with – she wore a tea gown, a looser garment that allowed her to dispense with the great

---

[1] He was, in fact, turned away twice. On the other occasion it was for arriving after 11 p.m., when the doors were firmly closed to latecomers. The patronesses of Almack's took pride in not caring whom they offended – an attitude that Her Ladyship would not advise her readers to adopt if they are looking for Social success in today's world.

A NOTE ABOUT MORNING DRESS

There was a time when the word 'morning' covered the period between breakfast and the evening meal: one of Jane Austen's letters, dated 1813, refers to breakfasting before nine and not dining until half-past six, 'so I hope we three shall have a long morning enough'. 'Morning dress' therefore described anything that was worn until it was time to change for dinner; and 'morning calls' were never paid before three in the afternoon. Modern English has lost this meaning but retains it in a word borrowed from French: at the theatre a *matinée* performance (literally, one given in the morning) could start as late as 5 p.m., with an evening one to follow.

The term 'morning dress' is no longer used for female apparel: only men wear it, at Royal Ascot, formal weddings and the like. It consists of a black or grey tailcoat with striped trousers; black or grey top hat; waistcoat and tie of reasonably restrained hue; and black shoes.

Although this book is aimed primarily at women, mention of black shoes reminds Her Ladyship that a gentleman should wear no other colour in town. Brown shoes go with tweed and, like tweed, should be worn only in the country. She also feels obliged to mention perhaps the worst of male sartorial solecisms: never, ever leave the top button of a shirt undone when wearing a tie. With an open-necked shirt (even if the openness extends no further than one button), take the tie off.

weight of whalebone that held her figure in place at other times of the day. Finally – or almost finally – came the evening dress: floor length with a flowing skirt, the bodice low-cut and with little or nothing in the way of sleeves. If she were going on to a ball she might change yet again or, more likely, wear her ballgown to dinner: it was more décolleté even than an evening gown and had a longer train that she would drape over her arm when she was dancing. (Modern fashion has improved on this: Her Ladyship recently attended a wedding where the bride's train had a loop that held it over her shoulder, leaving her arms free to indulge in today's more energetic dancing style.) Evening dress also included long gloves and quantities of the family jewels, which both showed off the wearer's status and indicated to a hostess that her guest considered her worth dressing up for.

Of course, fashions come and go. Vita Sackville-West's novel *The Edwardians* (1930) describes a recognised beauty in an opulent evening dress: 'oyster satin flowing out at her feet, pearls vanishing into the valley between her breasts, pearls looped round her wrists, a rosy scarf tossed round her shoulders'. But at the end of the Edwardian decade (1910) the designer Paul Poiret introduced a simple, high-waisted, uncorseted dress in much stronger colours than had previously been fashionable and would doubtless have dismissed oyster satin as insipid.

By the 1930s, a fashionable evening dress had a high neck but a very low back; in winter such a dress might have long sleeves, but the shoulders were left bare. Of necessity, then, there developed a fashion for chic jackets and wraps to stop the elegantly dressed from freezing to death. One pragmatic fashion columnist advised lining the sleeves of a jacket with 'a wafer-thin woollen' called domette, 'one of the warmest materials imaginable'.

The point, however, is that whatever fashion may have dictated, a young lady knew instinctively what the appropriate apparel was wherever she was going.

So what was she supposed to wear?

To court, in Victorian and Edwardian times, a short-sleeved white evening dress with a train. The colour proclaimed her virginity, though the fact that ivory and pale pink were also permissible encourages Her Ladyship to wonder whether some girls were more virginal than others. The train had to be between 2 and 3½ yards long (in today's parlance that is from just under 2 metres to just over 3). Also specified was the maximum length of the compulsory veil (no longer than 45in/115cm), held in place by a headdress of three white ostrich plumes carefully arranged in the style of the Prince of Wales feathers. Jewellery was unobtrusive: pearls were considered the most suitable adornment for debutantes. Married and older women could wear stronger colours and as much of the family jewel box as their necks and arms could bear.

The fact that ivory and pale pink were also permissible encourages Her Ladyship to wonder whether some girls were more virginal than others.

Even in court dress, however, fashion changed: by the end of the 1930s the ostrich feathers had gone and by the time of the last presentation, in 1958, debutantes were instructed – by the Lord Chamberlain, who issued the invitations – to wear 'day dress with hat'. Silk and chiffon were by then the fabrics of choice, with full skirts extending to just below the knee; less maidenly colours such as blue were perfectly permissible, though no doubt one or two dowagers clicked their tongues at things not being what they used to be.

Evening dress – which for men meant 'white tie and tails' – required a full-length gown, with a separate covering for the shoulders. For a 'black tie' occasion, women traditionally wore either an evening dress or a tea dress, reaching to below mid-calf and accompanied by gloves and a stole. A cocktail dress was less formal, reaching only to the knee.

As late as the 1940s ladies were expected to keep their gloves on even during dinner. These gloves, of white kid, had pearl buttons at the wrist so that the wearer could undo them, roll the 'hand' part back, tuck it carefully under her bracelets and leave her hands free to deal with knife, fork and glass. A lady would no more think of removing her gloves in public than she would of taking off her underwear – she would always carry out this potentially erotic act with great discretion, unless she was deliberately being seductive. In which case, of course, by the standards of the time she would have been no lady.

When it came to country house parties, the debutante also required suitable clothing for hunting, riding and walking. A 1930s newspaper fashion column advised travelling in a co-ordinating four-piece ensemble – cardigan coat, jacket, skirt and blouse – so as to leave the suitcase free for 'underclothing and night attire, a spare shirt or thin woollen jumper, a simple crepe day dress, an evening dress of printed chiffon or lace that can be packed into a small space without showing creases, heavy shoes for golf or walking, satin shoes for the evening, a beret or tricot cap, and a compact array of toilet requisites'. And this was an absolute bare minimum: most women would have preferred to take three or four evening dresses so that they did not commit the social solecism of wearing the same one twice. This is why, as J B Priestley observed in the passage already quoted (see page 13), they needed several trunks for even the shortest visit.

Modern dress codes

In many places – with the honourable exceptions of Royal Ascot and royal garden parties – dress codes are less rigid nowadays. Many use words such as 'customary' or 'recommended', but this still means that those who go too casually dressed are likely to be in the minority and therefore perhaps feel a bit out of place. Her Ladyship is one of those who feel that dressing up for a special occasion is part of the fun – and it is certainly a courtesy to your hostess if you are going as a guest.

Even today, the above guidelines generally hold good. A 'formal day dress' has a skirt that reaches at least to the knees and does not leave quantities of flesh exposed anywhere around or above the waist. At the lower end of the formality scale, 'smart casual' permits the wearing of tailored trousers, but implicitly or explicitly discourages jeans, shorts, tee shirts and trainers.

Finally, Her Ladyship would encourage her readers to bear in mind the words of Beau Brummell, great arbiter of style in Regency times: 'If people turn to look at you on the street, you are not well dressed.' Classic elegance rather than slavish following of fashion will always stand the debutante in good stead and a subtle sign of affluence will impress more people than flashing an ostentatious designer logo.

> *Her Ladyship would encourage her readers to bear in mind the words of Beau Brummell, great arbiter of style in Regency times: 'If people turn to look at you on the street, you are not well dressed.'*

Three

HOW TO BEHAVE

On with the dance! Let joy be unconfined;
No sleep till morn, when Youth and Pleasure meet
To chase the glowing hours with flying feet.

George Gordon, Lord Byron (1788–1824)

In addition to being well-dressed, a young lady was expected to be both 'pretty behaved' and 'accomplished'. Jane Austen, inevitably, expressed it best:

> *A woman must have a thorough knowledge of music, singing, drawing, dancing, and the modern languages to deserve the word [accomplished]; and besides all this, she must possess a certain something in her air and manner of walking, the tone of her voice, her address and expressions, or the word will be but half deserved.*

This is Miss Bingley in *Pride and Prejudice* (1813); Mr Darcy then adds, '…and to all this she must yet add something more substantial, in the improvement of her mind by extensive reading.' Small wonder that Elizabeth expresses surprise at their knowing *any* accomplished women.

The emphasis on modern languages is interesting. Travelling on the Continent – or least to Paris, even for women – was popular for much of the eighteenth century. The French Revolution, quickly followed by the Napoleonic Wars, then made it very difficult for ladies to go abroad, unless they were the wives of soldiers or diplomats. Well-bred girls were nonetheless expected

To be thought 'a bluestocking' or 'bookish' cast a damper over a girl's marriage prospects – Heaven forbid that she should be better read or better informed than her husband.

to be able to converse in French and, ideally, Italian. Anyone with any pretensions to scholarship would also have been well versed in the classical Latin and Greek authors, though to be thought 'a bluestocking' or 'bookish' cast a damper over a girl's marriage prospects – Heaven forbid that she should be better read or better informed than her husband.

Most upper-class girls in Jane Austen's day were educated at home by a governess; masters might be brought in for dancing and music, to prepare them for their coming out. Some girls were sent to select 'seminaries' or boarding schools where the turning out of young ladies of refinement was the single most important item on the curriculum.

Accomplishments versus education

Changes in the education system through the nineteenth century made it more common for girls to go to school and eventually even to university; nevertheless among the aristocracy the practice of keeping girls at home, at least during their early years, persisted. The writer Nancy Mitford, born in 1904, was educated at home until she was sixteen – although she admittedly had an eccentric father who claimed to believe that if his daughters went to school they would be forced to play hockey and would develop thick calves. Her Ladyship, who did go to school and did play hockey, would prefer not to comment on this. She cannot, however, resist the passing observation that the most beautiful of the famous Mitford sisters, Diana, (who was educated at home) achieved every debutante's (and certainly every debutante's mother's) dream by ending her first Season engaged to one of the Guinness family: in addition to being heir to a fabulous fortune, he had been to Eton and Oxford and was the grandson of two earls. In attracting a husband endowed with wealth, looks, charm and aristocratic connections, Diana had – as no one would have dreamt of saying in those days – ticked every possible box. The fact that the marriage ended after only three years, when she became involved with Britain's leading Fascist, Oswald Mosley, is, in this context, neither here nor there.

Whether or not they went to school, girls still had to learn to curtsey. For many years in the mid-twentieth century, *the* place to learn was the Vacani School of Dancing in Knightsbridge. Rows of future debutantes would hold on to the *barre* in Vacani's ballet studio and practise putting the left foot behind the right, leaning the weight on to the right foot, bending the knees, sinking down and rising up in one fluid movement. In the late 1930s girls were taught to bow the head only at the deepest point of the curtsey to the King and to smile as they rose. Then, bearing in mind that they would be wearing a long dress with a train, they practised the little kick that would prevent them tripping over their skirts as they moved three steps to the right and repeated the curtsey for the Queen. Dress rehearsals also prepared the girls for curtseying with the obligatory ostrich-feather headdress, and with their hands by their sides rather than grasping the *barre*. The royal curtsey was unhurried, elegant and respectful; the skirt-clutching bob of little girls at school prize-givings would not do at all.

The finishing touch

As girls' schools started to move closer to boys' schools in terms of the subjects on the curriculum, a vacancy occurred: girls who studied chemistry and geography still had to be turned into young ladies. Enter, therefore, the finishing school. Here social skills, deportment and elegance were the key skills. Girls who had just left school would often attend from September to March, by which time they would be deemed ready to make their way in Society – and their mothers would have organised everything to enable them to do so.

Although there was no shortage of finishing schools in London, some parents chose to send their daughters to similar establishments in Paris or in Switzerland where they would also perfect their French (an old habit dying hard). Finishing schools

still exist, though their curriculum now includes subjects such
as 'international etiquette and protocol', offering to prepare
women for their role in the business world as well as in society.

Much of this, of course, was and is a nightmare for a shy girl,
but teaching her to overcome her shyness – by equipping her with
the necessary social graces – was another function of finishing
schools. So, too, in the very early days of the Season, was allowing
her to attend small private parties before she officially 'came out'.
One matron in *Lady of Quality* (1972), a novel by Georgette Heyer,
the queen of Regency romance, put it this way:

> *I have frequently observed how often girls being...pitchforked straight
> from the schoolroom into the ton[2], ruin their chances by excessive
> shyness, which leads them to be tongue-tied, or – worse! – disagreeably
> pert, in the effort to appear up to snuff, as the saying is.*

Her Ladyship here draws her readers' attention to the turn
of phrase 'ruin their chances'. 'Put men off' would have been
another way of expressing the same sentiment.

Making conversation

Strict drilling in conversational topics may have been useful
for covering up shyness, but it had its drawbacks: J B Priestley
remarked that the talk throughout long lunches and dinners was
'vapid, the women prattling, the men uttering pompous nothings.
Any subject worth discussing was generally banned.' Eliza Doolittle
in *Pygmalion* – whom nobody could have accused of being vapid –
was warned to talk only about 'the weather and people's health'.

---

[2] Ton was a favourite Georgette Heyer word for 'high society'. Nothing to do with weights
and measures, it should be pronounced with a vaguely French accent, and rhyme with
'gone' rather than 'done'.

Yet, following the letter rather than the spirit of the instruction, she ended up discoursing on her aunt's death from influenza, her belief that the old woman had been 'done in' and her father's views on the remedial effects of gin. It was not what Mrs Higgins' guests were expecting to hear.

Priestley goes so far as to suggest that the restriction imposed on conversation was the reason so many of the apparently repressed and respectable Edwardians embarked on illicit affairs at weekend house parties – tiptoeing along the corridor to another bedroom was the only exciting thing that happened all day. Her Ladyship, who doesn't attend as many house parties as she used to, feels that this is perhaps not the place to expand on that potentially fruitful subject.

The modern debutante

Moving closer to modern times, the rules of conversation are less restrictive than they were a century ago, though it is still prudent to avoid those perennial pitfalls of politics and religion until you are certain that no one within earshot is going to be offended by what you say. Your views on the Mayor of London or the Archbishop of Canterbury may seem less reasonable when uttered in the presence of a local party activist or a vicar who has chosen not to wear his dog collar to a polo match.

Curtseying is also a less vital skill than it once was, unless you are meeting royalty. A shallower form of the Vacani curtsey will suffice for all but the most senior royals. Be warned, however: it is not easy to perform even a slight curtsey elegantly in high heels and

Take Her Ladyship's word for this, there is going to be someone around to photograph it – and publish it on what she believes is called Facebook – if you get it wrong.

a straight, knee-length skirt; and few things look more clumsy than a badly executed one. (And, please take Her Ladyship's word for this, there is going to be someone around to photograph it – and publish it on what she believes is called Facebook – if you get it wrong.)

If you are nervous about attending a High Society event for the first time, and don't have the time or financial resources to spend six months at finishing school, try breaking yourself in gently. For the horsily inclined, point-to-points are informal occasions for amateur riders, and provide an excellent chance to meet people throughout the country. There are point-to-point courses from Trebudannon in Cornwall to Dundee in Scotland – 116 in all in use for the 2012 season. Alternatively, if an event that tends not to have champagne bars and sheltered stands with closed-circuit TV is not your thing, get yourself invited to a hunt ball (see page 117) and practise moving gracefully in an evening dress and those impractical but undeniably fetching shoes.

Hunt balls are all very well, but there's no denying that many of the Season's most prestigious events revolve around sports, and outdoor sports at that. As Her Ladyship will indicate on various occasions later in the book, a little knowledge of any event you are attending will go a long way towards enhancing your enjoyment. If nothing else, it will give you something to talk about – at least until you can decently steer the conversation around to something else, and it will show your companions that you have made an effort.

Her Ladyship would hope that society in general has come a long way since then, but she does sometimes wonder whether Society has.

It would also be fruitless to deny that the Season was founded on the understanding that men would participate and women would watch, admire and, latterly, provide picnics. Her Ladyship would hope that society in general has come a long way since then, but she does sometimes wonder whether

Society has. If you have no interest in sport, can't cultivate
enthusiasm for opera or art, and aren't on the lookout for a
wealthy and well-connected husband, it is possible – and Her
Ladyship is as eager to sell her own work as any author, so does
not make this remark lightly – that this book may not be for you.

To sum up

Her Ladyship has four pieces of essential advice for young ladies
wishing to make their way in Social circles, and to enjoy to the
full the events described later in this book:

• Always dress appropriately. If you don't know what
'appropriately' is, ask your hostess or study the website for the
event in question. On many occasions, particularly outdoor ones,
common sense should take precedence over fashion. This applies
to shoes, coat, length of skirt and headgear. If you can't bear to be
seen in public in 'sensible shoes', don't accept an invitation to a

horse trial or the Braemar Gathering. And if you must wear stilettos, invest in some discreet 'heel protectors': these not only protect your shoes and any grass you may have to walk on, they also reduce the stagger factor in your walk and minimise the risk of your coming an undignified cropper on the dance floor.

• On formal-to-regal occasions an engraved invitation used to say, 'Tiaras will be worn.' Tiaras are still occasionally worn at weddings, official banquets and the like. But they should be worn only by married women and should be real and preferably heirlooms. As a perceptive article in *Country Life* put it, when an invitation to an appropriate occasion is received, 'there is a scrabble to beg, to borrow but almost never to buy a tiara'. Never, ever, except perhaps as part of fancy dress, wear a fake tiara – they are, in Her Ladyship's opinion, more vulgar than fascinators, and that is saying a great deal.

Never, ever, except perhaps as part of fancy dress, wear a fake tiara – they are, in Her Ladyship's opinion, more vulgar than fascinators, and that is saying a great deal.

• Balls and parties often end at four in the morning with some of their participants the worse for wear. See Her Ladyship's note about photographs on Facebook (page 38) and think very seriously about the consequences to your Social future before staggering out of a nightclub wearing only one shoe.

• Success in the Season requires you to receive invitations. Be the sort of guest that people will ask again. This does not necessarily mean you should offer to help with the washing-up in the Royal Enclosure, but such basic courtesies as:

- accepting an invitation (rather than turning up without having replied)
- making an effort to talk to other guests (even the older and less glamorous ones)
- thanking your hostess on departure (which should not be three hours after everyone else has gone)
- writing a thank-you note the following day (mentioning something specific to the occasion, such as another guest you enjoyed talking to, or your appreciation of the trouble your hostess had gone to)

will all gain you the reputation of being a desirable guest. From that, invitations will inevitably flow and then who knows how many husbands may follow?

PART II

Four

MARCH AND APRIL

*A horse is a thing of beauty... none will tire of looking at him
as long as he displays himself in his splendour.*

Xenophon (c. 435–354 BC)

Cheltenham Festival

Many non-traditionalists now regard this race meeting as the
start of the Season, though this may just be because it is a stylish
event that happens to take place in March, when the sap is rising
and people are starting to think about partying. Whatever else it
may be, though, the Cheltenham Festival is the highlight of the
jump-racing year. The Grand National, held a few weeks later, is
longer and the obstacles are larger, but the Cheltenham Gold Cup
is the race that earns accolades such as 'Blue Riband', 'jewel in the
crown' and 'most prestigious'. If 'prestigious' means 'lucrative for
successful owners', then this is unarguable: the prize money for
that one race is around £500,000.

'Prestigious' has a further meaning in this context, and the
novice racegoer eager to hold her own with more experienced
companions may like to memorise the following information. The
Cheltenham Gold Cup is the most valuable non-handicap race in
Britain. With minor adjustments for sex and age, all the horses
carry the same weight (whereas in a handicap race such as the
Grand National, horses that have done well in previous outings
carry extra weight). The handicap system is designed to make the

44

race fairer by giving every horse an equal chance of winning. A non-handicap (or 'level weights') race has no truck with fairness: it establishes which is the best horse in that category of race and thereby enhances both its own prestige and that of the horse.

In the case of the Cheltenham Gold Cup (you have to be careful not to confuse it with the Ascot one, see page 82), the prestige is enhanced by the nature of the race. Nothing less than a top-class thoroughbred steeplechaser will win it. The fences are demanding, the distance – 3 miles 2½ furlongs (or over 5km) – requires staying power and the final uphill stretch is, as modern euphemism would have it, challenging.

Your companions will be impressed if you know all this, but don't make the mistake of lecturing them: if they are at all interested in racing, they will almost certainly know it already.

Cheltenham adds to its reputation for generosity of prize money by producing a new Gold Cup every year. Her Ladyship regards this as highly commendable and wishes that she owned a successful racehorse. Containing almost 300 grams of gold, the Cup is worth about £8,500 in hard cash, never mind the craftsmanship, the glory of winning it and the fact that you don't have to give it back at the end of the year.

Cheltenham adds to its reputation for generosity of prize money by producing a new Gold Cup every year. Her Ladyship regards this as highly commendable and wishes that she owned a successful racehorse.

The Festival is also an early excuse to try out the best that your wardrobe has to offer. It runs from Tuesday to Friday and Ladies' Day is the Wednesday. In a recent innovation that Her Ladyship is inclined to think is vulgar but many others regard as fun, there are 'Fashion Awards', with prizes for 'best-dressed lady', 'lady with the best hat' and 'lady with the best accessories'.

Otherwise, although many ladies do wear hats during the Festival and gentlemen wear suits in the Club Enclosure and restaurants, there is no specific dress code: the weather at this time of year is too unpredictable for hard-and-fast rules.

Travel in style

Having started life at nearby Cleeve Hill in 1818, Cheltenham racing moved to its current location (in Prestbury, just outside the town) in 1831, the year after angry citizens – allegedly stirred up by the local priest – showed their disapproval of the evils of racing by burning the grandstand to the ground. The veneer of respectability that overlays English spa towns wore just a little thin on that occasion, some would say.

Local shuttle and charter helicopter flights or a helipad for your own machine are available – as, of course, are trains, buses, taxis and car parks. But the truly stylish way to travel here is by steam train. Embark at Winchcombe, where you will be entertained on the platform by an Irish band (there is no getting away from Irishness at the races – particularly at the Cheltenham Festival, which takes place very close to St Patrick's Day). You then spend half an hour puffing gently through idyllic Cotswold countryside, at a speed that might have been calculated to enable you to admire

the view. The train deposits you at the north entrance to the racecourse, just behind one of the grandstands. There is a licensed bar on board so, if the mood takes you, you can start early on the champagne – but remember that if you are entering the Ladies' Day Fashion Stakes you will have your photograph taken and you don't want to appear unbecomingly flushed.

Sadly Winchcombe Station is no longer on a commercial railway line – the link with Cheltenham has been restored by the heritage Gloucestershire Warwickshire Railway. But the people who organise 'classic hospitality' for the Festival have thought of that. If you don't want to drive to Winchcombe – or, more likely, don't want to drive back – there is a special bus service from the station to Moreton-in-Marsh, which has direct links with London Paddington. So you can relax, forget about traffic jams and travel the way Gold Cup lovers would have travelled a century ago.

As for husband potential, it is Her Ladyship's experience that all race meetings are immensely friendly occasions when it is easy to chat to strangers and she leaves her readers to take it from there.

The Boat Race

Not really part of the Season and included here only because of the opportunities it gives for mingling with young men from Oxford and Cambridge, the Boat Race was once a byword for undisciplined jollification. P G Wodehouse's Bertie Wooster, fined £5 for stealing a policeman's helmet on Boat Race night, later learned that he owed the leniency of his punishment to the fact that 'a certain licence is traditionally granted by the authorities' on this occasion. However, now that undisciplined jollification takes place across the capital on approximately 365 days of the average year, Her Ladyship would not advise Boat Race revellers to use the occasion as an excuse to get out of hand.

First rowed in 1829, the Boat Race has proved a surprisingly even affair over the years, with Cambridge five victories ahead of Oxford at the time of writing. That said, Oxford won 16 races out of 17 between 1976 and 1992 and still didn't quite catch up – Cambridge had a remarkably successful run some decades earlier, losing only one race between 1914 and 1936.

The race takes place on the Thames, between Putney Bridge and Mortlake, and covers a sinuous course of a little over 6km (3¾ miles). (Many non-Londoners assume that the Thames flows from west to east in a more or less straight line; in fact for a substantial part of the Boat Race course it flows due south and for another section due north.) A stone on the towpath below Putney Bridge marks the starting point but is unlikely to be visible on the day, thanks to the vast throng of revellers eager to see the boats off.

The Boat Race is in many ways an odd occasion – and was, even before protesters started swimming across the Thames to disrupt it. There can be few sports which attract such a massive audience on only one day of the year and whose excitement is over within twenty minutes. There are no tickets and no grandstands: you simply turn up and jostle for a place – early, if you want to watch the boats taking to the water and see the race between the two universities' reserve teams that precedes the main event. Vantage points at the start, on Hammersmith and Chiswick Bridges (respectively about the halfway point and near the finish) and at various boathouses along the way become very crowded very early in the day.

Despite the *ad hoc* nature of race-viewing arrangements, there is no shortage of entertainment. Specifically there is no shortage of opportunity to get yourself into the mood to steal a policeman's helmet. Her Ladyship urges you to remember that the authorities, not all of whom have been brought up on P G Wodehouse, are likely to have a zero-tolerance response to this sort of frivolity.

The Guineas

Newmarket is the home of racing, the place where Charles II established the sport in the seventeenth century. So keen was he that he moved the court to Newmarket twice a year to indulge his hobby; he also inaugurated the first ever official British horse race, the Town Plate, which is run at the July Festival to this day. Ardent racegoers can fill the two months between the Cheltenham Festival and the Derby by taking in the Season's first two 'classics' at Newmarket in late April or early May.

A 'classic' is, by dictionary definition, 'a traditional race, contest or sporting tournament having special significance and honorific value' and in British racing the term is applied to five flat races restricted to three-year-olds: the 1,000 and 2,000 Guineas, the Oaks, the Derby and the St Leger. It's worth noting the 'restricted to three-year-olds' part: three is the age when a flat-racing horse is generally at its peak and anyone who claims that the same horse won the Derby twice can confidently if tactlessly be accused of talking through his hat. The Guineas Festival lasts two days, with the 2,000 Guineas run on a Saturday and the 1,000 Guineas on a Sunday. The 1,000 Guineas is for fillies only; both sexes may run in the 2,000 Guineas, though fillies rarely do.

Fashion is not really a feature of the Guineas Festival – for that, in Newmarket, you need to wait for July. In the height of summer a three-day festival offers a Ladies' Day, billed as the region's most stylish event, on the opening day (Thursday). The fact that the July Festival is sponsored by a well-known brand of champagne helps to boost the party atmosphere.

A practical note

There are two important things to remember about Newmarket: don't go overdressed to the Guineas Festival (smart casual, with no jeans or trainers in the Premier Enclosure, is recommended); and make sure you go to the right place. Despite having a population of only about 15,000 people, this passionately racing-dedicated town has two courses. The Rowley Mile is used for the Guineas Festival, other spring meetings and in the autumn; the July Course for summer racing.

The two courses are very different. The Rowley Mile traces its ancestry back to the time of Charles II – the name comes from his favourite horse, Old Rowley, which came to be a nickname for the king himself. It has been likened to Lord's and Wimbledon in terms of its position at the heart of its sport: high-quality races are run on 'the most historic stretch of turf in the entire world of sport'. Facilities at the July Course were much refurbished a few years ago, but the old-style grandstands were retained and the overall feel is much more intimate, fostering the 'garden party' atmosphere that is integral to the July Festival.

Newmarket is not ideally situated for public transport, but the racecourse provides a coach service to and from Cambridge station on race days. The premier car park can be booked in advance, but both courses also offer free parking slightly further away. As at many other venues, it is worth wearing comfortable shoes and, if necessary, changing when you get to the enclosures.

A Pastoral Interlude:
Palace Garden Parties

With the number of young ladies wishing to be
presented at court becoming unmanageable by the
1940s, Royal Presentation Garden Parties were instituted,
to be deemed by Society to 'count' as a presentation. Since
the abandoning of court presentations in the 1950s, the
parties have broadened in scope. There are at least three
a year at Buckingham Palace and one at Holyroodhouse
in Edinburgh, entertaining about 10,000 people each
time. An extra party may be given for a special reason: in
1997, for example, on the occasion of the golden wedding
anniversary of the Queen and the Duke of Edinburgh,
invitations were extended to couples who were celebrating
their own golden wedding. Bands play, tea is served in large
tents and the royal party circulates for two hours and chats
with people on a pre-arranged list. At Buckingham Palace,
it is worth getting there early – the gates open at 3 o'clock
and royalty doesn't make its appearance until 4 – if you
want the chance to wander around the gardens, which
are never otherwise open to the public.

It is worth noting, though, that there is very little
shade; men in particular, in their morning dress, can suffer
on a hot day. One friend of Her Ladyship's, honoured with
an invitation to a garden party when the temperature was
hot enough to wilt sandwiches and melt chocolate icing,
was very relieved to discover that there was ice cream
discreetly on offer in another tent and advises anyone
else so stricken to seek it out.

Instructions on parking will be sent with your invitation, though the palace is a short walk from Victoria Station and an easy taxi journey from anywhere in central London. (The queue for a taxi to take you home may be lengthy, though: you may prefer to cajole a non-republican friend into picking you up.) The dress code is smart day dress and hat – beware of stiletto heels that will sink too far into the regal lawn. And Her Ladyship cannot resist the temptation to relate a true tale of a fashion embarrassment that a friend experienced at a Palace Garden Party many years ago.

A talented seamstress, Her Ladyship's friend made her own dress for the party. It was green and to accompany it she concocted a white hat (on a base bought at a popular department store) adorned with a matching green silk rose. Unfortunately, shortly before the party, a friend came to admire the dress, bringing with her a small daughter who promptly spilled ice cream over it. The green dress being now unwearable, the only suitable alternative Her Ladyship's friend possessed was a black one, so she substituted the green roses on the hat with black ones,

The look on the Princess's face would, in an earlier century, have sent Her Ladyship's friend to the Tower with instructions to throw away the key.

bought from the same department store. Imagine her horror when Princess Margaret emerged into the Palace garden, wearing what looked like exactly the same hat. It seems unlikely that

Her Majesty's sister's headgear had been cobbled together at the last minute from supplies bought at John Lewis, but Her Ladyship's friend assures her that the resemblance was striking. Her horror, it must be added, was nothing to that of Her Royal Highness: the look on the Princess's face would, in an earlier century, have sent Her Ladyship's friend to the Tower with instructions to throw away the key.

This can hardly be described as a cautionary tale, as there is no moral to it – unless it is to be more careful about letting small children with ice cream come anywhere near your wardrobe.

To return to the point...

The purpose of the Royal Garden Parties is to recognise public service and achievement: names of those who may deserve an invitation are put forward by Parliament, the armed forces, various charities and other such bodies. To many of the events in this book, you may be able to blag an invitation (as Her Ladyship believes the expression is) from a well-connected friend, or simply to splash out lots of money for a ticket. To be invited to a Palace Garden Party, you need to do something meritorious. Which may be no bad thing.

Five

MAY

'I suppose society is wonderfully delightful!'
'To be in it is merely a bore. But to be out of it simply a tragedy.'
Oscar Wilde (1854–1900)

Chester Festival

There was a time – perhaps fifty or a hundred years ago – when no debutante could possibly have fitted the Chester Racing Festival into her schedule unless, perhaps, she lived in Chester. It takes place in early May, when she would have been far too busy preparing for her court presentation, her own ball and attending the dances given for all her friends.

Now that this particular form of pressure is less intense, the Festival is a good excuse for a day out in pleasant spring weather. Ladies' Day (on day two of a three-day meeting) is also likely to be a more clement opportunity than Cheltenham to try out the frocks, hats and shoes that may or may not cut the mustard at Ascot in June.

The highlight of the meeting for racing fans is the Chester Cup, which has been contested, though not always under that name, since 1824 and is seen as an important precursor of the Derby the following month and the St Leger in the autumn.

Sadly, the last horse to achieve the Chester Cup/Derby double was Shergar in 1981; this may be a precedent that contemporary racehorse owners are loth to follow.

That said, Chester is not only a beautiful course, it is the oldest in Britain. Racing here goes back to the time of Henry VIII, well over a century before Charles II took his (various) pleasures at Newmarket. It was introduced to replace a football match, which was considered to have become too violent. Her Ladyship – not a football fan – passes on this legend without comment. The town's history dates back a lot further than that, and more of it is coming to light, with evidence of Chester's importance as a port in Roman and medieval times. Her Ladyship advises anyone wishing to impress their racegoing companions to brush up on the course's latest archaeological findings before their visit.

Badminton Horse Trials

A three-day event lasting five days? Well, why not? All the more time for socialising.

Badminton House – which sits in beautiful parkland in southern Gloucestershire – is the ancestral home of the Dukes of Beaufort; in fact, the manor has been in the family since before the dukedom was created in 1682. The house itself was remodelled in the eighteenth century, when the architects James Gibbs and William Kent gave it the Palladian look that it retains to this day. It is not open to the public, although anyone who has seen the film *The Remains of the Day* will be familiar with its entrance hall, butler's and housekeeper's parlours and conservatory. The gardens are open – by pre-booked tickets only – on three days of the year.

Horse 'events' have been held here since 1949 – they were inaugurated by the then Duke, a keen horseman and Master of the Horse for the Royal Family, after he had visited the 1948 London Olympics. His idea was to provide British riders with somewhere to train for international events: Great Britain's track record in subsequent Olympic Games and World and European Championships shows just how successful the venture has been. The first year attracted 22 entrants from Britain and Ireland, with a prize purse of about £500. Today the maximum number of horses competing is 85 and, despite the high standards horses and riders must achieve in order to qualify, there is always a waiting list; in 2011 the total prize money was over £250,000. In other words, Badminton is recognised as among the most prestigious (and certainly one of the most testing) three-day events in the world.

The trials are held over a long weekend (Thursday to Monday) in early May and the key events are the dressage (to display the horse's 'obedience, discipline, accuracy and elegance') on Friday and Saturday, the cross-country on Sunday and the show jumping on Monday. Equestriennes wishing to improve their competitive skills can pay a small fee (£15 at the time of writing) to walk the cross-country course with a professional rider and learn how to tackle the different fences. At the risk of bringing a blush to maidenly cheeks, Her Ladyship should also mention the Stallion Display on Saturday afternoon, though she prefers to remain vague about exactly what is being displayed. More modestly but very endearingly, Sunday morning offers the Shetland Pony Grand National.

At the risk of bringing a blush to maidenly cheeks, Her Ladyship should also mention the Stallion Display on Saturday afternoon, though she prefers to remain vague about exactly what is being displayed.

Practicalities

Admission to the ground allows you access to unreserved
seats for the dressage and to the temporary grandstands on the
cross-country course. Additional tickets are required for reserved
seating to watch the show jumping and these sell out very quickly,
so shop early.

Public transport to Badminton is very limited, although
coach transport from Chippenham, the nearest railway station,
can be arranged. Even though Badminton is only about 10km
(6 miles) from the M4, the approach roads are likely to be
congested from very early in the morning. Those wishing to
avoid the traffic often take the option of arriving by air. Having
booked in advance, they may then land on the runway, located to
the west of the lake in front of Badminton House, from where it
is an easy walk to the course. Helicopters may arrive at any time,
though a phone call in advance to the Aircraft Office is essential.
On cross-country day, aircraft must land before 11.45 a.m. and are
not usually permitted to take off before 5 p.m. On other days they
are forbidden to fly over the main arena when show jumping or
dressage is in progress. This seems to Her Ladyship to be only
courteous: there are many ways in which considerate people
will restrain themselves so as not to frighten the horses.

Dress code: 'Smart casual or country wear is appropriate.
In particular, sensible walking shoes are strongly recommended!'
says the website. Her Ladyship adds that the presence of an on-site
camping and caravan site encourages even greater informality, and
that jeans and even shorts with training shoes are a frequent sight.
Badminton, for all its many charms, is not the place for designer
stilettos, nor for the sort of frock that would grace Ascot.

Chelsea Flower Show

On payment of a modest subscription, anyone may become
a member of the Royal Horticultural Society. Among the
advantages of membership is free entry to the Society's four
gardens: Wisley in Surrey, Hyde Hall in Essex, Harlow Carr in
Yorkshire and Rosemoor in Devon. Her Ladyship can vouch
personally for the beauty of three of these places; she rarely visits
Essex, but has no reason to suppose that Hyde Hall is any less
lovely than its sisters. But while a visit to any of these gardens may
be an enjoyable family day out or a charming walk in cultivated
surroundings, the Chelsea Flower Show is the most prestigious
event in the gardening calendar; and another advantage of
membership of the RHS is that it allows you to purchase tickets
at a discount and to attend the show on your choice of two days
before the general public is admitted.

The RHS Great Spring Show dates back to 1862 and has been
held in the gardens of the Royal Hospital, Chelsea, since 1913. The
Society itself was the brainchild of John Hatchard, whose bookshop
still occupies the premises on Piccadilly where the idea came to
fruition in 1801. It has enjoyed royal patronage since 1816, when
it attracted the attention of Queen Charlotte – she to whom the
whole concept of the Season owes such a great debt of gratitude.

The show runs for five days in May. The Royal Family and
horticulturally minded celebrities visit on Monday, before it opens
to anyone else; then there are two days for members only before
the general public is admitted for the final three. Attractions
include the famous display gardens in the outdoor area.
These purport to set or reflect the latest trends, though they do
sometimes stretch beyond the aspirational and into the fantastical:
not everyone, even in the wealthier stratum of Her Ladyship's
acquaintance, is likely to install a mountain stream or sculpted
columns in their garden. For the more down-to-earth there are

magnificent exhibits of flowers, plantings and exotic crops in the Great Pavilion – covering some 1,500 square metres, it has appeared in the *Guinness Book of Records* as the world's largest tent – and numerous trade stands where you can buy anything from a flowerpot in the shape of an elephant to an umbrella in the shape of a chrysanthemum.

Not everyone, even in the wealthier stratum of Her Ladyship's acquaintance, is likely to install a mountain stream or sculpted columns in their garden.

Avoiding the crowds

The exclusion of the general public does not stop members' days being packed to the gunwales (the total number of visitors over the five days tops 150,000). Those with a genuine interest in gardens and gardening should buy 'all day entry' tickets and arrive as early as possible (from 8 a.m.): by lunchtime it is almost impossible to obtain a reasonable view of the show gardens or to walk along the main pathways at anything faster than a snail's pace – an unwelcome analogy at a flower show. Cheaper tickets allow admission only after 3.30 or (cheaper still) 5.30 p.m., which means that the afternoons and evenings can become very crowded indeed.

The 'go early' rule does not apply to the last day, when from 4 p.m. exhibitors sell off unwanted plants and accoutrements at prices that turn respectable dowagers into candidates for bull-running in Pamplona. Her Ladyship shudders to contemplate the behaviour of some of her acquaintances, who cast decorum to the four winds in order to acquire a medal-winning foxglove past which royalty strolled a few days earlier. One piece of advice gleaned from a veteran of these anarchic afternoons: if you can possibly find a place to park, drive. It isn't easy to fit a treasured piece of topiary into the overhead luggage rack of the average commuter train.

Reverting to the days on which one does conduct oneself with decorum, those with no interest in gardens and gardening should arrive early enough to guarantee a comfortable seat in the Pimm's tent, or stay away altogether.

Dress code: as the RHS rules forbid the use of coloured statuary, no garden gnomes are admitted (though at least one frequent exhibitor is known to have smuggled some in). Other than that, dress is practical: thanks to the vagaries of the British spring, many of the pathways are either dusty or muddy and most people favour comfort and practicality over elegance. It is, in any case, a rare hat that can compete with Chelsea's displays of roses, lilies and irises.

It is, in any case, a rare hat that can compete with Chelsea's displays of roses, lilies and irises.

If not Chelsea…

Those who feel that Chelsea has become uncomfortably crowded may prefer to wait for early July in order to visit the more spacious RHS show at Hampton Court. Although it has been going only since 1990, it is the world's largest flower show, covering over 13 hectares and attracting 600 exhibitors, many of them rose specialists. As at Chelsea the first two days (of six) are for RHS members only; but members and non-members alike may purchase tickets to a preview evening where they can view the gardens and displays in a relaxed atmosphere, enjoy a picnic or dinner and finish by watching a firework display over the Thames.

The RHS also hosts shows in Cardiff (April), Malvern (May), Tatton Park, Cheshire (July) and the London Horticultural Halls (February, March, April and October). Few people would go to any of these specifically for their husband potential, but on the other hand they provide the perfect opportunity for a man you've never met before to act on impulse and give you flowers.

Glyndebourne Festival Opera

David Hockney, who has designed a number of sets for this most famous of opera festivals, has said that many English people probably imagine Heaven as being a bit like Glyndebourne: a beautiful setting with strains of Mozart wafting across the lawn. He doesn't mention the clink of champagne flutes, but Her Ladyship would argue that they have their place in Heaven too. They certainly have their place at Glyndebourne.

The Festival's history is romantic. In 1930 a 29-year-old soprano called Audrey Mildmay was engaged to take part in a production of Mozart's *Il Seraglio* in the splendid Organ Room at John Christie's country home on the North Downs in Sussex. Christie was in the habit of staging amateur performances for an invited audience of family and friends, with a few professional artistes thrown in. Described as a Pickwickian eccentric, and certainly at 48 considered a confirmed bachelor, he astonished all who knew him (and perhaps not least himself) by falling instantly in love with Audrey. They were married within six months and together realised his dream of mounting productions on a larger scale. The first theatre, begun when the Christies returned from their honeymoon, seated 300 people and opened in 1934 with a season consisting of two more Mozart operas, *Così fan Tutte* and *The Marriage of Figaro*.

The current building, opened in 1994, seats 1,200; more to the point, for music lovers, it has superb acoustics and attracts world-class professional singers, musicians, directors, designers *et al.* As one supporter puts it, 'There's going to the opera – and there's going to Glyndebourne.'

The Festival runs from late May to late August and always features six operas, of which three are new productions (and, not infrequently, new operas). The productions run in rep format rather than consecutively, so it is possible to go three times in the same week and see three different works. So yes, you can go to Glyndebourne for the opera, and if opera is your passion you are unlikely to be disappointed. But if opera is not your passion, you are unlikely to be disappointed either.

Glyndebourne's gardens

The gardens are everything you might expect from a country house that has been there (if not entirely in its current form) since Elizabethan times. They boast walled gardens and parterres, spectacular herbaceous borders and a rose bower as well as generous expanses of lawn. Across a wire fence from the lawn sheep may safely graze; they may also stare at your picnic without making you feel that they are likely to make inroads into the smoked salmon while your back is turned.

In addition there is a lake around which you can take an agreeable and surprisingly peaceful stroll – it constantly amazes Her Ladyship how few of the British public choose to venture more than 50 metres from a car park, even on the balmiest day. It is worth arriving early not only to secure the best spot for your picnic but to give yourself plenty of time to enjoy the grounds.

The gardens are a joy throughout the Festival season, though May, when the irises are at their peak, is perhaps Her Ladyship's favourite time. The occasional tree scattered across the lawn provides much-needed shelter from sun or rain, according to nature's whims – while Her Ladyship is sure that there are days at Glyndebourne when the weather could be described as moderate, she seems only ever to have been on very sunny or very wet days.

Practicalities

The schedule for each day's programme is geared to the time of the last train back to London, so it varies according to the length of the opera but is always an hour and a quarter earlier on

Sundays. 'First bell' may therefore be as early as 3.30 p.m. or as late as 6.15 p.m., with the performance ending at 9.40 p.m. (8.25 p.m. on Sundays). If the piece is long enough to warrant it, there will be a short interval (15–20 minutes) after the first act. But there is always the famous 'long interval' of 85 minutes half to two-thirds of the way through, and this is when Glyndebourne really comes into its own for the less passionate opera-goer. Bring your own picnic, picnic furniture, linen tablecloth and napkins, bone china, silver ice bucket, champagne flutes, Pimm's jug and anything else you may feel is required to make the interval go with a fizz. If by any chance champagne is not your drink of choice, do remember other necessary accoutrements: Her Ladyship's party was once accosted by an impeccably black-tied but suitably embarrassed gentleman asking if he could borrow a corkscrew.

While some say that catering for yourself is the best option, there are those who swear by the Glyndebourne traditional picnic: a three-course meal, ordered in advance, which can, if desired, include champagne, porter service and suitable furniture. Her Ladyship advises against penny-pinching here: unless you are *very* young, picnicking on the ground is uncomfortable and whatever your age there is a tendency for the champagne to fall over. Why not hire furniture and have pleasant young men to wait on you when the opportunity is offered?

A NOTE ABOUT PICNICS

Many people treat their Glyndebourne picnic as an annual ritual and set high and glamorous standards: 'no Tupperware' is a common rule, but Her Ladyship has one friend who insists on bringing the family silver for cutlery and serving spoons. This is very much a matter of taste, as are the contents of the picnic hamper itself, though your local delicatessen will probably be only too happy to advise – and to supply ready-made *bonnes bouches* – if you are unsure of your own abilities. Alternatively, there are mail-order companies that will take the problem entirely off your shoulders.

If you do choose to go it alone, Her Ladyship would offer these few words of advice:

• Don't prepare anything that is going to be soggy by the time you want to eat it. This tends to include anything with tomatoes or cucumber in it, whether it be sandwiches or salads. Take the ingredients separately and, as long as you remember to bring a sharp knife, the fruits can be sliced quickly and crisply just as you are ready to eat them. Similarly, don't add salad dressing until the very last minute.

• Give thought to the heat (or lack of it) of the day. Soup in a wide-mouthed thermos is a godsend when the weather is really cold. On the other hand, on a hot day, beware of poisoning your guests with prawns that have been baking in the boot for three hours. Invest in insulated cool bags and bins; if you add ice packs to them they should keep food pleasantly cool all day.

• Notwithstanding the above, some foodstuffs are asking for trouble in hot weather. Avoid chocolate, cheesecake and anything else of a consistency that is going to be a gooey mess after ten minutes in the sun.

• Don't forget the odds and ends that make all the difference: salt, pepper, mustard, ginger for the prawns, perhaps a nice chutney if you are serving cheese or cold meats. Also plenty of napkins, a bag or two for rubbish and a cloth with which to wipe dirty plates before packing them away.

• Make sure you have enough cutlery for serving, including butter knives, cheese knives and a pie or cake server if necessary. Nothing takes the gloss off a picnic more than having to help yourself to strawberries with a spoon tainted with mayonnaise.

If you prefer not to picnic, Glyndebourne has three restaurants for a sumptuous afternoon tea before the performance and/or dinner in the long interval. These must also be booked in advance: remember that there are likely to be over a thousand people in the grounds, all of them anxious to eat and drink their fill before the same starting time and during the same 85-minute 'window'.

As for dress code, the website has this to say:

> *The tradition of wearing evening dress during the Glyndebourne Festival originated with founder John Christie, who felt that it was one of the ways the audience could show its respect for the performers.*

Evening dress of black tie for men and a long or short dress for ladies is customary for the summer Festival.

Hats (for women) may complement an outfit and be desirable on hot days, but are not *de rigueur*, while morning dress with top hat would be decidedly over the top. Although there are a few sheltered places to picnic if it rains, even these are likely to be chilly, so a sensible outer garment is advisable.

Trains from London Victoria take just over an hour (to Lewes) and are met by the Glyndebourne chartered bus – free of charge, but book your place when you book your ticket. The return coach departs half an hour after the performance ends. And, just in case you feel that your dress will be damaged or your feet miserable if you travel in your finery, Glyndebourne thoughtfully provides a changing room near the car park.

This may all sound very efficient and straightforward, but none of it matters unless you have a ticket. Glyndebourne is much sought after. On payment of an annual fee you can become an Associate Member, after which you are likely to wait ten years before being offered the opportunity to become a full Member. Festival Society Members and Associate Members are offered priority booking before Christmas; tickets are subsequently made available to those on the Festival Mailing List. Sadly, this is currently full, so if you don't number a subscriber among your acquaintance, you will have to take your chances when booking opens to the public in late March. Be warned – popular productions such as Mozarts sell out quickly.

Glyndebourne around the country

There is no getting away from the fact that opera tends to
be a recreation for the comfortably off. Two performances
each season are designated as part of the Glyndebourne<30
programme, which means that 500 tickets per performance are
available at substantially reduced prices to those aged under 30.
Otherwise, the best seats for the Festival operas are almost £200.

Those who reel at this fact and/or do not have ready access
to East Sussex may prefer to support Glyndebourne on Tour. This
begins with three weeks at Glyndebourne in the autumn and visits
seven other venues round the country, with a programme of three
operas; there is also the opportunity to see a current production
'live' or a recent production 'captured live' in selected cinemas.
Prices begin at a level that most people would find manageable,
but do go high enough to accommodate opera snobs who like to
feel they are indulging in an élite hobby. For those watching a
production 'live' who feel that 85 minutes is quite a long interval
at the cinema: fear not, the organisers have thought of this. They
start the live transmission a bit after curtain-up at Glyndebourne,
have a half-hour interval and synchronise their broadcast so that
the last act is indeed live. None of this has the 'Social Season' feel
of the Festival itself, but is useful for those – and there are some –
whose priority is to hear the operas.

Not a great deal of mingling goes on at Glyndebourne; there
is a tendency to stick with one's own party. So the unattached can
relax, revel in the very special atmosphere and ponder the
thought that there are worse things in life than being fancy
free in an English summer.

Although Glyndebourne is the largest and the longest
established, England is now blessed with a number of other
beautiful venues for summer opera and these are listed under
Garsington on page 79.

Six

JUNE

Summer afternoon – summer afternoon; to me those have always been the two most beautiful words in the English language.

Henry James (1843–1916)

Eton: the Fourth of June

The future King George III was born on 4 June 1738 and his birthday is the reason for the slightly bizarre annual 'open day' held at Eton College. The king spent a lot of his time at nearby Windsor Castle and was closely associated with the college; Eton's first riverside pageant, with fireworks, was celebrated in his honour in 1793.

Although the original festivities were probably held precisely on His Majesty's birthday, Eton's Fourth of June is now a moveable feast.[3] In the past the date has been specified as either the Wednesday after the second bank holiday in May or the Wednesday before the first weekend in June – which in most years comes to the same thing. In 2012, however, just when people thought they were beginning to understand the system, it was celebrated on 2 June, which was a Saturday. Her Ladyship would

[3] Older readers may remember the critic Clive James's memoir of his time at Cambridge: entitled *May Week Was in June*, it also pointed out that May Week lasted a fortnight. So the fact that the Fourth of June almost never falls on 4th June puts it in good company.

not usually demean herself to use the expression 'Go figure', but she feels it is quite appropriate here. Check the Eton website before preparing your picnic.

The centrepiece of the day's entertainment is the Procession of Boats, which features the school's top rowing crews, dressed – in another respectful nod towards George III – in naval uniforms of early nineteenth-century design, including straw hats garlanded with flowers. The crews row one at a time past the crowds assembled on the riverbank. The members of each eight then stand up in the boats and salute the guests with their oars. Strict sobriety for the oarsmen is advised, as chorus-girl synchronicity is required and this is no mean balancing act even without having to combat the effects of Buck's Fizz.

This is no mean balancing act even without having to combat the effects of Buck's Fizz.

Guests at the Fourth of June are parents and 'members of the College community'. The best way to gain an invitation, therefore, is to have a brother at Eton or to number obliging Old Etonians among your friends. The latter at least should not be difficult, as they seem to be everywhere – or so Her Ladyship feels every time she watches the television news. Weather permitting, picnics and light summer frocks are the order of the day.

Royal Academy Summer Exhibition

For many years the Season 'began' at the private view of the Royal
Academy's Summer Exhibition in late May. Never mind the fact
that Court presentations might have taken place two months
earlier and cocktail parties and dances would have been in full
swing for weeks – the Summer Exhibition made it official. One
1950s debutante Fiona McCarthy, in her book *Last Curtsey: the
End of the Debutantes* (2006), assessed it frankly:

> *Not that the paintings themselves were the focus of attention in
> what was less an exhibition than a huge midday cocktail party
> without cocktails, a gathering of the aristocracy and diplomats,
> the politicians, artists and literary figures who comprised the
> then establishment.*

The company had been every bit as elite in Victorian times,
when the artist William Frith produced a satirical painting entitled
A Private View at the Royal Academy 1881. In it he depicted, among
many other famous faces, Oscar Wilde holding court on the
subject of the art on display; he also showed a number of elegant
ladies whose dresses proclaimed a slavish adherence to transitory
fashion. 'I wished to hit the folly of listening to self-elected critics
in matters of taste, whether in dress or art,' Frith explained.

Her Ladyship cannot help but raise a tiny side issue here.
Is it William Frith, critic of ephemeral fads, or Oscar Wilde, who
maintained that a little sincerity was a dangerous thing and a
great deal of it absolutely fatal, who is a household name today?

No matter. The Preview Party, as it is now called, remains
a glittering, celebrity-studded occasion (the dress code is
encapsulated in the single word 'glamorous'). Other things have
changed, though: it tends to be in early June, is held in the early
evening, a lot of the guests are pop stars and there is no question

of it being cocktail-free. It used to be by invitation only; nowadays you can apply for tickets via the Fundraising Events page of the Academy's website and congratulate yourself on making a generous donation to an estimable institution which receives no state subsidy.

In addition to its traditional role as a 'see and be seen' occasion, the party also provides art lovers with the opportunity to purchase some of the 1,400-plus works on display, before even the invited buyers have their chance. It has to be said that 1,400 pictures is *a lot* for a single exhibition, so despite the glamour of the party it really does help to have cultivated at least a token interest in art.

Husband potential: dazzling. There is absolutely no knowing whom you might meet.

The Derby

The world's most esteemed classic horse race, the Derby is one of many examples of the British aristocracy's obsession with horseflesh. Goodwood is another, whereas without royal patronage neither Ascot nor Newmarket would be where it is today (socially speaking, that is – the towns themselves would presumably be in the same place). The Derby was founded by a sporting peer, the Earl of Derby, in 1780 and has been run every year since. Unlike many of the Season's events it was not suspended during the two World Wars; it simply and prudently moved from Epsom, its peacetime home, to Newmarket. Other races and sporting competitions bearing the name 'derby' – from the horse race in Kentucky to, Her Ladyship is reliably informed, a football match between Birmingham City and Aston Villa – all take their name from this one. Only Americans, doubtless justifying themselves by the fact that Kentucky is closer to home than the south of England, refer to 'the Epsom Derby'.

The Derby Festival is held over two days, with the Derby itself run on the first Saturday in June. The Oaks – named after the Earl of Derby's estate in Surrey and first run a year before the first Derby – is on the Friday.

Like the 2,000 Guineas and the St Leger, the Derby is open to both sexes, though at Epsom fillies generally enter the Oaks just as at Newmarket they enter the 1,000 Guineas. There is a theoretical Triple Crown of the 2,000 Guineas, the Derby and the St Leger, but it has been won only once since the Second World War – by Nijinsky in 1970. Nowadays it is comparatively rare for a Derby winner to enter the St Leger: the latter, being a longer race, requires more stamina and, according to one school of thought, a Derby winner's enormous stud value would be lessened by a poor performance at the St Leger. It is extraordinary, Her Ladyship cannot help but observe, just how much of life boils down to sex. Even if you are a horse.

Ladies' Day

Although the Friday is designated Ladies' Day, the dress requirements are more stringent for Derby Day itself. In the Queen's Stand on Ladies' Day you are merely asked to wear a fascinator or hat; on Derby Day the headgear is required rather than requested, the fascinator must be substantial and the rest of your costume must be a formal day dress or a tailored trouser suit. Gentlemen can content themselves with a suit and tie on Friday; on Saturday it is black or grey morning dress with a top hat. As elsewhere, jeans, tee shirts, fancy dress and other such indications that you are not treating the occasion with respect are forbidden.

All that said, the ladies' hats that appear on Derby Day tend to be elegant but quietly spoken. Ladies' Day does produce its share of feathers and frivolity, but nothing to compare with the fantastical creations of Royal Ascot.

Getting there

It is easy to reach Epsom by public transport, and the organisers encourage it. There are three stations nearby and a bus shuttle service runs from Epsom (not Epsom Downs) station to the course during the Derby meeting. Be aware, though, that literally hundreds of thousands of people will be having the same idea over the two days of the Festival. As Her Ladyship seems to be saying for almost every event in this book, go early.

As for husband potential, it's not bad. You are in Surrey, after all.

Garsington Opera

Opera lovers who like an excuse to dress up and parade around country estates are twice-blessed in the English summer. Not only can those who choose to do so visit Glyndebourne six times in the space of three months, but for an intense four-week period in June and early July they can also take in three different operas at Wormsley in Buckinghamshire. That remark brings Her Ladyship quickly to the single most important thing to remember about Garsington Opera: it no longer takes place at Garsington.

There is a (little) history behind this odd statement. Garsington Opera is a mere child by the standards of most of the events in this book, having been founded as recently as 1989 by the then owners of Garsington Manor in Oxfordshire, Leonard and Rosalind Ingrams. Once the home of the Society hostess Lady Ottoline Morrell, Garsington hosted many a literary gathering in the height of the 'Bloomsbury' days, with Virginia Woolf, Lytton Strachey and T S Eliot among the visitors. Lady Ottoline herself was responsible for the design of the gardens in which early productions of Garsington Opera were held.

After Leonard Ingrams' sadly premature death in 2005, the family decided to seek a new venue for the opera and in 2011 the company held its first performances in its new home.

Wormsley, owned by the Getty family (which, Her Ladyship assumes, needs no introduction), is a country estate in the great English tradition, with words such as 'rolling' and 'verdant' tripping off the tongue whenever anyone attempts to describe it. The pavilion in which performances take place looks out over deer park, lake and woods. Designed to be erected and dismantled each year, it is Japanese-inspired, light, transparent and intimate. As at Glyndebourne, operas begin in late afternoon and have a long interval in which guests – who are encouraged to wear evening dress – may dine in one of the marquees, picnic in the extensive grounds or stroll around admiring, among other things, the cricket pavilion.

Yes, cricket pavilion. In addition to being a great philanthropist, the late John Paul Getty II, father of the current owner, was a great Anglophile. In particular, he loved cricket and he had a replica of the Oval Cricket Ground built in Wormsley's grounds. International and other cricket takes place here throughout the summer, with Brian Lara, Imran Khan and Andrew Flintoff among the players who have appeared in charity matches. The grounds are available for hire for corporate and other events, but a number of cricket matches are open to the public every year.

Another of the attractions of Wormsley is the walled garden. It covers about three-quarters of a hectare (2 acres to those of an old-fashioned turn of mind), which makes it substantial by walled-garden standards. Not normally accessible to the public, it is open in the afternoon of opera days and opera-goers who arrive early may be taken there in a shuttle bus.

Other summer opera

Mention of walled gardens reminds Her Ladyship of another lustrous opera venue – **West Green House**, near Hartley Wintney in Hampshire. On a smaller scale than Garsington, it offers two operas, each for two nights only, in July, in one of the loveliest gardens in England. The so-called Green Theatre is under cover but the sides are open to the air, allowing patrons to enjoy the gardens and the spectacular lighting that comes into its own as the sun goes down and the last act begins. Interval picnics may be taken in the orangery or the pavilions around the lake. The backdrop of an eighteenth-century house whose façade looks, as its website says, like a set for *The Marriage of Figaro*, puts West Green near the top of the list for those who choose their opera according to the visual splendour of its setting.

Last but by no means least as a venue for 'country-house opera' is **Grange Park** in Hampshire, with a programme of five operas running for about six weeks in June and July.

A modest seventeenth-century house in the park once served as a hunting lodge to the Prince Regent, but in the early nineteenth century this was knocked down and rebuilt as a Grecian temple – the first 'Greek revival' house in England. At the time it belonged to a member of the Drummond banking family; he sold it to a Baring, also of banking fame, and it has remained in that family – now the Barons Ashburton – ever since. The first festival took place in 1998 in the orangery of the house; since then a 550-seater theatre has been built inside the orangery to provide such luxuries as wings, which mean that the singers no longer have to clamber over scaffolding to re-enter stage right having exited stage left.

Glorious grounds for picnicking, a stately home in the background, champagne in specially erected pavilions, the opportunity to dress in your best – Grange Park may be a newcomer on the operatic scene, but it has made sure that it has all the desirable ingredients on tap. It has also taken the view that the simple attractions are sometimes the best: as one friend of Her Ladyship's put it, 'You can drink champagne anywhere, but the Grange's afternoon tea [served on the balcony overlooking the grounds] is something special.' Its dress code even offers scope for the imagination: although evening dress is preferred, men who do not choose to wear black tie may opt for 'any stylish alternative'.

One word of warning, however: the car park is in a field. Wearing something practical and carrying your evening shoes with a view to changing them when you reach dry land is a good idea on inclement days.

VERONA

Opera lovers who find the emphasis of the English Season
too sporting may choose at some point to make an excuse
and leave for the delights of a Roman amphitheatre in
northern Italy. Since its inception in 1913 – the centenary
of the birth of the great operatic composer Giuseppe Verdi
– the Arena di Verona Festival has taken place in the largest
and most spectacular open-air theatre in the world.
Spectators are required to dress 'in an elegant manner,
appropriate to a theatre venue', though Her Ladyship
regrets to say that she has seen visitors of both sexes dressed
in jeans. More important, though, is to treat the monument
itself with respect – and to wear shoes appropriate to
clambering up and down its steep stone steps.

The first ever production at the festival was Verdi's
spectacular, cast-of-thousands *Aida* and this still features in
the repertoire more often than any other work. There are
those who say that you haven't really been to Verona if you
haven't heard *Aida*, but failing that there are always six
productions to choose from, including some popular,
entry-level operas such as *Carmen* and *Don Giovanni*. The
season runs from late June to late August or even early
September, so the jaded Season-goer has plenty of choice
over which home-grown events to miss. If anyone says to
you reproachfully, 'My dear, I didn't see you at Henley (or
the Open or Cowes),' the bubble of their disapprobation
will be well and truly pricked if you are able to say that you
popped over to the Arena di Verona for the weekend.

Royal Ascot

Regarded by many as being at the very top of the Social tree, Royal Ascot runs for five days (Tuesday to Saturday) in the third week of June. Much of the fun of Ascot is that every day is 'fashion statement' day, but, as the website puts it, 'Although the whole week of Royal Ascot is a fashion show like no other, it is Thursday when the designer creations and millinery masterpieces reach new heights.' Over the years, hats in the form of wedding cakes, floral displays, macaws in flight, flamenco dancers and Big Ben, the London Eye and the Gherkin (all in one) have put more conventional confections to shame; no aspirant to fashion would turn up to Royal Ascot wearing nothing more imaginative than a vast array of purple feathers. Even the impeccable Cecil Beaton designs for *My Fair Lady* would seem a little tame by today's standards.

No aspirant to fashion would turn up to Royal Ascot wearing nothing more imaginative than a vast array of purple feathers.

Low and high points

Those who were appalled at a drunken brawl breaking out in the Royal Enclosure at Ascot in 2011 may like to know that sticklers have considered that standards have been slipping for almost a century. In 1921 it was reported, in shocked tones, that some ladies wore the same dress on two consecutive days; by 1924 some were even wearing sleeveless dresses, exposing vaccination marks (more prominent and even less attractive then than they are now) to a disapproving world. In more recent years Her Ladyship has noticed a distressing tendency, on the part of many young women attending Ladies' Day, to squeeze themselves into dresses that look more like negligées that are several sizes too small; to dress so scantily that on a cool day they display an unattractive quantity of gooseflesh; to wear fake tan that has omitted to cover their feet and ankles; and to become so drunk that they have to stagger back to the car park holding their ill-chosen shoes – none of which adds to the distinction of the occasion. As a friend of hers tersely put it, 'I don't expect them to have ladies' maids to help them dress, but you'd think they would look in the mirror before they left home.'

However, with any luck, these strictures have become a thing of the past. In 2012, aware that, to use their own words, there had been 'misunderstanding of what constitutes appropriate attire for this formal occasion', the organisers of Royal Ascot announced revisions to the dress code for visitors to the Royal Enclosure. The code has always been fairly strict and quite specific – midriffs are to be covered, mini-skirts are inappropriate – but they are now even more so. Women have to wear hats – and by hats, they mean hats, not fascinators. Or – because the guidelines are very clear – 'a headpiece which has a base of 4 inches (10cm) or more in diameter is acceptable as an alternative to a hat'. Strapless tops or those with skimpy straps are banned; skirts are to be of 'a modest length', with just above the knee being the shortest permissible. For the men cravats are prohibited; black or grey morning dress, with top hat, waistcoat and tie are *de rigueur*. This is, the organisers say, both a clarification of what formal attire means in the modern world and a deliberate attempt to restore formality, which they believe most of those attending the occasion relish.

Applications for tickets for the Royal Enclosure are accepted only from those sponsored by an existing member who has attended on four previous occasions. If you insist on wearing a fascinator (though Her Ladyship does beg you to reconsider), you may do so in the Grandstand Enclosure: here, hats or fascinators are now compulsory, where previously they were merely encouraged.

If you insist on wearing a fascinator (though Her Ladyship does beg you to reconsider), you may do so in the Grandstand Enclosure.

The Royals at Royal Ascot

Royal Ascot is – even by the standard of events in this book – extremely royal. The Queen has not missed a meeting for 65 years and, rather than putting in a token appearance, she attends for four days. Each day begins with the Royal Procession, a tradition that dates back to the 1820s: members of the Royal Family and honoured guests arrive in a parade of horse-drawn landaus – open-topped carriages whose roofs can, as a last resort, be pulled up if the weather is intolerable. Bearing in mind that even the most exclusive of race meetings involves gambling, bets at Royal Ascot are taken not only on the horses but on the likely colour of Her Majesty's hat.

The Gold Cup

Speaking of horses, there are plenty of them for those who can tear their attention away from the fashions. The big race is the Gold Cup, inaugurated in 1807 and run over 2 miles and 4 furlongs (just over 4 kilometres). This is a long distance in the flat-racing world – appreciably longer than either the Derby or the St Leger – so the Gold Cup is a race for 'stayers' and is the most prestigious such race in the world. Purists would never dream of calling it the Ascot Gold Cup, any more than they would describe the golfing 'major' as the British Open or the classic horse race as

the Epsom Derby. There may be other events the world over with these names, but the lack of further description implies – quite rightly, in Her Ladyship's view – that the Gold Cup, the Open and the Derby are the originals and still the best.

Getting there – and back

As for getting to Ascot, in the event of not being invited to arrive in a landau: parking must be pre-booked at the same time as tickets are purchased ('early to avoid disappointment', as with most of the events in this book). The racecourse is close to both the M3 and the M4, the latter meaning that access from the M40 and M25 is also easy. Bear in mind, however, that some 300,000 people will be visiting in the course of the week. The Royal Ascot website advises that the local roads are likely to be congested by 11 a.m. (the Royal Procession is at 2 p.m. and the first race at 2.30) and Her Ladyship advises anyone wearing shoes in which they can manage a seven-minute walk to come – early – by train. That said, one friend made the mistake of joining an overcrowded train at Clapham Junction rather than Waterloo; she then had the unpleasant experience of travelling for five hours through five counties to accomplish a journey that is normally scheduled to take 44 minutes.

Arriving early is all very well, but it doesn't avoid the problem of almost everyone wanting to leave at the same time. One solution to this is to miss the last race (or two) and depart *before* the hordes; perhaps a better one is to take a light picnic and eat it in the car park while waiting for the worst of the traffic to die down.

The car park is some distance from the course, so Her Ladyship does – as so often – recommend comfortable shoes (which can be changed when you arrive). Her experience is that, far from eyeing you askance, the car-park attendants will compliment you on your sound common sense.

The Championships

Not many people – even those who assiduously look at the logo on television every day for a fortnight each year – are aware that this is the proper name of what is generally known as Wimbledon. But so it is. Taking place at the end of June and beginning of July, these are the oldest and most prestigious lawn tennis championships in the world. There have now been over 125 championships held here. The first – men's singles only – was played in 1877; women started competing as early as 1884. 1877 was also the year when the All England Croquet and Lawn Tennis Club formulated a new code of laws for tennis.

Another thing that not many people will know is that before then the game was administered by the Marylebone Cricket Club or MCC, whose Tennis and Racquets Subcommittee had drafted the first laws of lawn tennis two years earlier.

Wimbledon is also the oldest of the so-called Grand Slam tournaments. Perhaps surprisingly, though – given that the British seem to have been the pioneers of most great sporting events – it does not pre-date the others by much. *Wimbledon's grass remains the doyen of international tennis, and its championships the ones that everyone wants to win.* The precursor of the US Open was first played in 1881, the French in 1891 and the Australian in 1905. But even though many, many tournaments across the world are now played on clay or hard surfaces, Wimbledon's grass remains the doyen of international tennis, and its championships the ones that everyone wants to win.

You have to be on the ball (no pun intended) to obtain tickets for the show courts at Wimbledon – the majority of them are sold by public ballot, for which applications close in December, some six months before the event. As is to be expected, demand much exceeds supply and disappointment is likely. However, there are other possibilities: some tickets are allocated to tennis clubs and to individual members of the Lawn Tennis Association, so you improve your chances of being able to spectate if you take the game up actively. Ballots for these tickets are held on a club-by-club basis between late March and May and the rules about 'uptake' and paying for tickets promptly are strict. So if you are going to be away over Easter, brief someone else to act on your behalf in the event of your being successful.

As a third option, some tickets are available online the day before play. Sign up on the Wimbledon website to receive email updates for the best chance of obtaining these.

Finally there is what is known as 'The Queue'. As queues go it is decidedly regimented: you are given a dated and numbered card to show your position in it; the police and local authorities give permission for people to queue overnight and the Honorary Stewards of the Championships operate a Code of Conduct in the event of disputes. But it does mean that a lucky few hundred people will be able to buy tickets for the show courts on the day of play – an unusual state of affairs for an internationally acclaimed sporting event, most of which sell out months in advance.

No such pressure applies to admission to the ground, however. Tickets are much easier to come by and, during the first week at least, you have every chance of seeing some top players on the 'outside' courts.

Even now that Centre Court has a retractable roof, the Great British summer weather can play havoc with the schedule, so it is never possible to guarantee what match you are going to see. This can, however, work to your advantage: a friend of Her Ladyship's, with scant interest in the ladies' game, was invited to Ladies' Finals day and, thanks to the rain that had fallen earlier in the week, was also treated to a delayed men's semi-final between, as it happened, the two top-ranking players in the world.

So what is all the fuss about?

Well, tennis is one of the few spectator sports offering equal enjoyment to both men and women. Men are able to admire the preternaturally long legs of many of the female competitors, while on a warm day women can nurture the hope that male competitors will want to change their shirt whenever they change ends.

Oh dear. Her Ladyship apologises for that digression. She had left the file open on her computer and a teenaged visitor saw fit to add that undignified comment.

In fact, Wimbledon is about great tennis and, as the cliché has it, it's also about strawberries and cream, possibly washed down with a glass or two of Pimm's. In the course of the two weeks that the championships run, some 200,000 glasses of Pimm's are sold, not to mention 28,000 kilos of strawberries.

Getting there

As with many Seasonal events, public transport is strongly recommended. Parking is limited and cars parked illegally in the adjacent streets will be towed away; the Wimbledon website also advises that the All England Lawn Tennis Club's postcode will confuse the sat-nav. There is no dress code, other than that dictated by common sense – sun hats or extra jumpers depending on the weather and whether you are likely to be sitting in sun or shade. Light permitting, play continues well into the evening, so be prepared for temperatures to drop. Wimbledon frowns on unlicensed advertising and spectators are expressly forbidden to wear the branded sun hats and rain capes often handed out to those waiting in The Queue.

Husband potential? Not great – most people do come to see the tennis. On the other hand, players give interviews and do signing sessions in the Aorangi Pavilion, so the chances of a brief encounter with a celebrity are attractively high.

On a smaller scale

…but almost as venerable, having been established in 1886, the Queen's Club hosts a star-attracting pre-Wimbledon tournament at its headquarters in just-west-of-central London. Tickets may be purchased for ground admission only, or for a designated seat on one of the two show courts. The charm of **Queen's** lies precisely in its small scale: even on Centre Court you feel very close to the play.

Queen's is proud of the fact that it was the first multi-sports centre built anywhere in the world, and it also plays host to the World Real Tennis Championships in late April. There is much to recommend a visit here, including the fact that a week of social events, including a black-tie dinner, is planned to coincide with the championships. In addition, you will learn (if you don't know already) that there is nothing unreal about lawn tennis but that the 'real' of real tennis means 'royal'; and, if you choose your seat wisely, you will watch the matches from the area known delightfully as the Dedans. Further study will tell you that real tennis is also known as the *jeu de dedans* ('inside game'); that the sloping roof areas of the huge indoor court are called penthouses; and that the sport was popularised in Britain by Henry VIII. The court at Hampton Court where he played was refurbished in the time of Charles II and the game is still played there. Given that many people spend the Season doing precisely the same thing as everyone else, Her Ladyship feels that these pieces of comparatively arcane knowledge, used discreetly, will greatly enhance your conversational powers.

Henley Royal Regatta

The late Sir Clement Freud, MP, journalist and bon viveur, wrote in *The Times* of his visit to Henley in 1996: 'Had my hair been long, my coat ribboned, collar winged, cravat pink, trousers white, boots made of buckskin, with a boater upon my head, buttonhole in my lapel, striped umbrella in hand – no one would have given me a second glance.' Henley undeniably has its own eye-catching style and is perhaps the only one of the events described in this book where the men, with their bright rowing-club blazers and boaters, are more splendidly dressed than the women.

'Had my hair been long, my coat ribboned, collar winged, cravat pink, trousers white, boots made of buckskin, with a boater upon my head, buttonhole in my lapel, striped umbrella in hand – no one would have given me a second glance.'

The dress code for the Stewards' Enclosure follows long-established tradition and is strictly enforced. Gentlemen must wear lounge suits, or jackets or blazers with flannels, and a tie or cravat. Ladies are required to wear dresses or skirts with a hemline below the knee and will not be admitted wearing divided skirts, culottes or trousers of any kind.

Hats (for women), though not insisted upon, are generally worn. The website adds the following kindly but firm warning:

> *Members are particularly asked to bring the dress code to the attention of their Guests [the capital letter is the website's], to ensure that the standards are maintained and to avoid the possibility of embarrassment of a Guest being refused admission.*

Gentlemen are not allowed to remove their jackets until an announcement is made granting them permission to do so;

this sometimes seems to happen only just in time to prevent both jackets and wearers from melting in the heat.

Officials wearing bowler hats patrol the enclosure to enforce the dress code and also to prevent anyone from using a mobile phone – the only place at Henley where a mobile is permitted is in the lavatories.

Henley's lavatories have another interesting feature. The final day of the Regatta – a Sunday – often coincides with the Men's Singles Final at Wimbledon or some other major sporting event. Progress reports on these are posted in the men's – but not the ladies' – lavatories. Or so Her Ladyship, not having seen the evidence of this for herself, is reliably informed.

To return to the subject of dress, admission to the Stewards' Enclosure is restricted to members of Henley's prestigious Leander Club and their guests; non-members wishing to attend the regatta may purchase tickets for the Regatta Enclosure, where a similar standard of dress is encouraged but not enforced. The purse-pinched may take a picnic, walk along the Thames towpath to a convenient spot and watch for nothing – the course, starting from the famous Temple Island, is over 2km (1¼ miles) long, and the grandstands and enclosures don't occupy all of it. Such spectators will, however, miss out on the fun of feeling involved – and they won't be anywhere near the finishing line.

The less purse-pinched may apply (well in advance, places are limited and sell out quickly) for moorings on Fawley Meadows and watch the racing from the water. Here, blazers and boaters are still the uniform of choice for most men and the atmosphere is decidedly relaxed.

The truly wealthy may hire the Temple on Temple Island for corporate hospitality or private parties. This eighteenth-century folly was inspired by designs that had recently been discovered in Pompeii and reflects the passion for things Italianate and Classical that wealthy young men brought back from the Grand Tour. The only way to reach the island is by boat, which adds greatly to the glamour – and also perhaps the folly – of the whole experience.

The racing itself

Henley Royal Regatta offers some 200 races over five days in late June or early July. There are twenty events at various levels, with crews ranging from one to eight in number; unusually for a regatta of this kind, only two boats compete, on a knock-out basis, in each race. Races begin at five-minute intervals and take about seven minutes, so although there is scope for 'blink and you'll miss it' anxiety, there is also the comfort of knowing that there will be another one along in a moment. In the 'open' races – the highest level – the rowing is of international standard, with champions past, present and future from all over the world taking part. As Wimbledon is to tennis, so Henley is to rowing: whatever their background or speciality, everyone wants to be here and everyone wants to win.

A practical note...

Her Ladyship advises readers to arrive by public transport if at all possible. The station is within easy walking distance and an enhanced rail service from London runs during the Regatta. For motorists, there is parking available (buy a permit in advance), but Henley is a small and old town with roads designed for pedestrians and a complicated one-way system that changes direction in the middle of the afternoon. One friend of Her Ladyship's tells a horror story of having taken five hours to cover the 20km (12½ miles) from the nearest motorway junction. With a start every five minutes, that means missing a lot of races.

Some of the car parking is fifteen minutes' walk from the Steward's Enclosure, but there is a cloakroom outside the enclosure where large bags must be deposited. Her Ladyship recommends walking in comfortable shoes while carrying your dressy ones, then leaving the comfortable ones in the cloakroom for the day.

Also, the same advice as she gave for Royal Ascot applies here: at the end of the day, everyone will be wanting to leave at the same time. Take a picnic or plan a stroll round the town before returning to your car, to let the worst of the traffic die down.

...and a snobbish note

The Regatta began in 1839 as a public fair in which rowing played only a small part. The rowing quickly increased in importance and since 1851, when Prince Albert took an interest in it, the Regatta has had a royal patron. Yet somehow the stigma of the 'public' entertainment lingered: in the first decade of the 20th century, according to Vita Sackville-West (who knew more about the *haut monde* than most people), the truly High part of High Society didn't go to Henley. Those who hanker after elitism should not be deterred, however: by 1947, when the Regatta resumed after the Second World War, society diarist 'Jennifer' was remarking that it was nearly as difficult to obtain an invitation to the Stewards' Enclosure as it was to get into the Royal Enclosure at Royal Ascot.

As for husband potential, with only four of the twenty events being for women, up to thirty-two boats competing in each event and up to eight rowers in each boat... Her Ladyship frankly cannot face doing the sums, but it adds up to a lot of very athletic young men. The teenaged visitor who made the inappropriate comment about Wimbledon on page 88 recommends those whose tastes run in this direction to find a way into the Boathouse, where strapping oarsmen, minimally clad in Lycra, are to be seen in abundance.

A Scottish Interlude

Edinburgh has always had its own social whirl, running in parallel to the London-based one but also continuing later into the year. In the spring and early summer an excursion to the Perth races in Scone Palace Park was and is a high spot, with its history dating back to the seventeenth century and the legend that Bonnie Prince Charlie took time out from planning the 1745 Rebellion in order to go racing (or perhaps surreptitiously to meet his co-conspirators) there. Today Perth is host to the Caledonian Gold Cup (early June) and has a Ladies' Day (mid-May) whose hats rival those seen at Cheltenham or Goodwood.

Many British racecourses are in beautiful settings; Perth is probably the only one to share its turf with land where generations of kings were crowned. Both Robert the Bruce and Macbeth were crowned in Scone Abbey, on the famous 'Stone of Scone'. This, readers may remember, later sat in Westminster Abbey for seven centuries and caused rumbling discontent between the English and the Scots. The English returned it in 1996 and it now resides in Edinburgh Castle alongside the Scottish Crown Jewels. A replica can, however, be seen on Moot Hill in Scone Palace Park, which neatly brings Her Ladyship away from that digression, back to Perth races and the Season.

As the centrepiece of the Edinburgh Season, the Queen spends a week at the end of June and beginning of July at what is officially known as the Palace of Holyroodhouse, carrying out engagements there; until the 1950s those engagements included court presentations. The very last debutantes to be presented to Her Majesty were therefore the Scottish ones – on 3 July 1958, several months after their English counterparts. Nowadays, during Holyrood Week, a garden party is held at the palace, as is an investiture for Scottish residents who have been recognised in the latest Honours Lists. The Holyrood Garden Party has, as one might expect, a Scottish flavour – the bands playing include pipers – but otherwise the 'form' is much the same as at Buckingham Palace (see page 51), and the same credentials of good deeds are required in order to receive an invitation.

In Scotland, coming-out balls were traditionally held around this time – again, later than in England. Some Scottish debutantes would, however, go south from March onwards and take part in the traditional events; English girls, following the movement of the Court, would go north in late June and be invited to the Scottish balls, so there was considerable overlap between the two Social circles. In London, North met South as early as the end of April at the **Royal Caledonian Ball**, a grand occasion that originated in the 1840s when the Duke and Duchess of Atholl decided to give a party for their London-based Scottish friends. Within a very few years this had become an annual 'subscription' dance, with invited guests making a donation to Scottish charities; over 150 years on, the Royal Caledonian is probably the oldest charity ball in the world.

For all that it is held in the Grosvenor House, Park Lane, the ball is a highlight of the Scottish calendar: formal Highland dress (clan sashes for the ladies) is compulsory for those wishing to participate in the 'set reels' which form a substantial part of the evening's dancing.

There is no need to be recommended by a committee member for the Caledonian Ball: just pay your money, learn the reels, arrive correctly dressed and prepare to enjoy yourself – energetically.

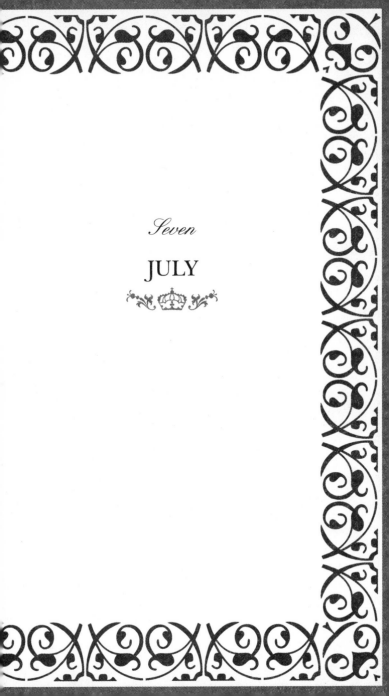

Seven

JULY

Cricket to us was more than play,
It was a worship in the summer sun.

Edmund Blunden (1896–1974)

The Lord's Test

There is no Ladies' Day at Lord's, although at least women are now allowed to be members and are therefore permitted in the Pavilion. (Until 1998, the only females allowed in were the Queen and the domestic staff.) But the dress code is token compared with that of other events: even trousers are permitted, provided they are accompanied by blouses and 'appropriate' shoes. And no such restrictions apply to those watching the game from the stands.

On an average Test day, women are in a minority of roughly one in fifty (Lord's is one of very few places where Her Ladyship can guarantee there will be no queue in the ladies' lavatories – Ascot on Ladies' Day can be uncomfortable in this respect). The men and the television cameras alike concentrate on the game. There is, therefore, no reason on earth to put on a fascinator and high heels. Not even the other women – most of whom are there because they are cricket fans – will notice.

In other words, in Social terms, the Lord's Test is – to use a somewhat inappropriate cliché, given the amount of alcohol that is often consumed there – pretty small beer. Even the description 'the Lord's Test' is, in most years, both faintly anachronistic and confusing: the demands of modern international cricket are such that, in the course of the summer, England frequently plays host to two touring teams. As most make a five-day appearance here, the average summer sees two Lord's Tests. To the further irritation of those trying to plan a Social calendar, they are not even at predictable times – in 2011 they were in early June and late July; in 2012 in mid-May and mid-August.

None of this is in any way intended to downplay the joy of the occasion, which Her Ladyship happens to love. Players always say that Lord's is a special place – like Wimbledon for tennis and Henley for rowing, it is *the* ground where they want to appear and to do well. It is cricket's spiritual home and its owner, the Marylebone Cricket Club or MCC, presides over the Laws and Spirit of the game. The Spirit (the reverential capital letter is always used) is in fact incorporated into the Laws. Her Ladyship thinks that this is a unique attribute of cricket and can't help feeling that some other sports might benefit from adopting it.

However, she does acknowledge that there are those who don't share her passion for cricket. If you recoiled at the earlier reference to 'five days' (for yes, that is how long a Test match lasts) she hastens to console you with the information that it is not compulsory to arrive on Thursday morning and remain, come rain or shine, until Sunday evening. You buy a ticket for one day and come and go on that day as you please.

Some practical points

Major matches (notably Tests featuring Australia, and any one-day international) are generally oversubscribed. Members of the public may enter a ballot for tickets in January. Membership of the MCC entitles you to early-booking privileges, but to become a member, unless you are an accomplished cricketer of either sex, requires not only the backing of four existing members but also the willingness to wait an estimated eighteen years for your name to reach the top of the waiting list.

Cricket is notoriously baffling to newcomers and those who do not understand the game may, if they choose, study the 'explanation for foreigners', most commonly found printed on tea towels. This begins, 'You have two sides: one out in the field and one in. Each man on the side that's in goes out, and when he is out he comes in and the next man goes in until he is out.' There is much more in this vein – for some reason cricket seems never to have inspired anyone to write anything short. But as not everyone will find this explanation as clear as it might be, Her Ladyship can reassure her readers that the Lord's crowd is both well-informed and friendly: there is no embarrassment in asking the complete stranger sitting next to you what is going on. Not only that, but the pace of the game is such that the novice can digest her neighbour's patient reply without missing much of what is happening on the field.

Other cricket at Lord's...

Her Ladyship further acknowledges that there will be those for whom the pace of a five-day match is just too slow. She feels that this is a shame, as the whole point of cricket is its leisureliness, but admits that even it must move – slowly – with the times. For those who have fallen victim to the hectic atmosphere of the twenty-first century, therefore, Lord's also hosts one-day internationals, the finals of domestic one-day competitions, the Oxford vs Cambridge Universities match, the Eton vs Harrow match, 20-20 matches (which last not much longer than a football match that goes to extra time), Middlesex and MCC home games and many more other cricketing events besides.

The Eton–Harrow match, formerly played over two days, used to be a highlight of the Season: 'Jennifer's Diary' in 1947 mentioned over seventy socialites who were present; by the early 1990s, 'Jennifer' recorded sorrowfully in her memoir, there would probably not have been seven. The match 'has lost status socially, and is now a very unsmart one-day affair, with a very poor attendance'. Her Ladyship leaves her readers to analyse precisely what 'Jennifer' meant by 'poor attendance', but feels reasonably certain that she was not referring to the *number* of people present. The shocking suggestion that Eton and Harrow would abandon Lord's altogether and play their match at the two schools in alternate years has, however, not yet come to pass.

...and elsewhere

Nor – though some members of the MCC would view this as heresy – is Lord's the only cricket ground in the country. Venues for Tests vary. The Oval in south London is almost always on the list and has its claim to venerableness: it hosted the first Test match in England, in 1880, four years ahead of Lord's. In fact – and Her Ladyship makes no apology for inundating her readers with this information, because cricket more than any other sport has a statistic for every occasion – the first Test match of all was not even played in England, but at the Melbourne Cricket Ground, and Test cricket had made its debut in Sydney and at Old Trafford in Manchester before it reached Lord's.

For a century or more, apart from a never-repeated diversion to Sheffield in 1902, Test matches in England were played at only six grounds: in addition to the three already mentioned, there were – and still are – Edgbaston (Birmingham), Trent Bridge (Nottingham) and Headingley (Leeds). Venues in Durham, Cardiff[4]

---

[4] Whatever its political status, Wales counts as England for cricketing purposes.

and Southampton have been added since 2003; in a year when there are two touring teams it is likely that at least one international match will be played at each of the above (and two at some). Again, Test matches and one-day internationals are likely to sell out quickly, so readers are advised to keep an eye on the various websites for schedules and ticket availability.

Husband potential on any of these occasions is not great, except for the purely statistical fact that men outnumber women so comprehensively. Those who love cricket tend to love it obsessively and to have little attention to spare to discuss anything except the game with chance-met females. But, with the greatest possible respect to the Braemar Gathering, the Season is intrinsically an English institution and there is no more English way of spending a summer's day than at a cricket ground – any cricket ground, even one on a village green – with a glass of wine in hand and the glorious summer game unfolding, oh so gently, before your eyes.

> *The Season is intrinsically an English institution and there is no more English way of spending a summer's day than at a cricket ground.*

British Grand Prix

Her Ladyship does not wish to be disparaging about any of the Social events of the Season; she realises that some people enjoy watching paint dry and admits that they have every right to do so. That said, she hopes her readers will forgive her if, when it comes to motor racing, she confines herself to the factual.

The British Grand Prix takes place at Silverstone in Northamptonshire on a Sunday in early July; the meeting lasts three days, with the big race as the climax. The race, and the cars competing, are designated 'Formula 1'; the 'formula' refers to the set of rules to which cars must conform (there are also Formulas 2, 3 and 4, built to lower specifications). Only Formula 1 cars, the fastest and the best at cornering, are allowed to take part in Grand Prix races.

What happens when

The Friday of the Silverstone meeting has practice sessions; on Saturday there is the qualifying race in which drivers compete for the coveted 'pole position' – whoever records the fastest lap time in the qualifier has the honour of starting in the best place on the 'grid'. In addition, there is a full programme of racing, with smaller cars competing for less prestigious trophies. But as these smaller cars often include legendary marques or rare classics, there is plenty for the motoring enthusiast to enjoy. On Friday and Saturday there is also the opportunity for those with three-day grandstand tickets to wander freely, taking a seat in whatever stand appeals to them or investigating the many trade stands and car displays. There is always the chance of bumping into a celebrity in the course of these strolls, but even falling into conversation with less famous fellow racegoers can have pleasing results. One friend of Her Ladyship's cherishes a photograph of himself sitting at the wheel of a Formula 1 McLaren car; he was allowed this privilege for no better reason than that his mobile phone bore the name of one of the sponsors. In addition to having pride of place on his mantelpiece, this picture gives him a pleasing sense of superiority over those who boast that their mobile provider gives them cheap cinema tickets.

Entry to the pits is by invitation only, but invitations can be won in competitions held on the day. This happened recently to a nine-year-old acquaintance of Her Ladyship's who returned from claiming his prize having met two of the leading drivers and clutching a tee shirt bearing both their signatures. The way his enthusiasm bubbled over compared favourably with anything a Grand Prix winner could do with a bottle of champagne.

A little history

Readers who have studied the time-honoured pedigrees of many of the events described in this book may be surprised to learn that the British Grand Prix is not the oldest event of its kind in the world. Alternatively, they may give a moment's thought to the name and draw their own conclusions. The French invented motor racing as early as the 1890s and the first race to be called a Grand Prix took place in Le Mans in 1906. It was held over two days, with six laps of the 103km (80¾ mile) course on each day. Each lap took roughly an hour, adding up to a total race length of over 12 hours. Having promised to stick to facts (and having already confessed her enthusiasm for the five-day form of cricket), Her Ladyship will record without comment that the first trophy awarded for a motor-racing victory was called the Gordon Bennett Cup.

Getting there

The British event began in 1926 and for some time moved between venues, including Brands Hatch and Aintree; it has been based at Silverstone only since 1987. Since then, the local roads have become notorious for their traffic jams at Grand Prix time and those in the know arrive by helicopter. From about 5.30 a.m. on the Sunday a constant stream of helicopters may be heard shuttling an equally constant stream of racegoers to the track. The flight from regional airports such as Elstree and Denham (both conveniently placed for London and Heathrow) takes less than half an hour; flights are also available from airports across the country. These land you only a few hundred metres from the circuit. Alternatively, you can make your way to nearby Turweston Airfield and be transferred to the circuit cross-country in a 4x4 vehicle – via a route rendered all the more exciting by being a closely guarded secret.

Unless you are invited to join some organised hospitality in one of the restaurants or private terraces, there is no dress code at Silverstone. It isn't that sort of event. As for husband potential – take your own and expect not to see much of him all weekend.

As for husband potential – take your own and expect not to see much of him all weekend.

An out-of-Season note

Although the event originated in Europe, with Spain and Italy alongside France and Britain as early holders of Grand Prix races, there are now some twenty races in the Formula One World Championship. Enthusiasts can globetrot even more intensively than those who chase around after solar eclipses. You can take in Grand Prix in Australia and Malaysia in March, or in Abu Dhabi, the United States and Brazil in November, without missing any of the home-grown Seasonal events. Alternatively, if you lost money at last year's Derby and don't want to repeat the experience you could take yourself to Canada in June, while in September the Singapore Grand Prix could provide a handy excuse for not joining a partridge-shooting party.

Cartier International Polo

The naming of this event is potentially confusing: sumptuous jeweller Cartier is the principal sponsor, the hosts are the Guards Polo Club in Windsor Great Park and the event's official name is the Hurlingham Polo Association's International Day. (The HPA is the MCC of polo – the headquarters of the game, its official governing body in the UK and Ireland and the arbiter in matters of sporting conduct.)

Whatever you choose to call it, it is the same thing, *the* big event in the polo year, attracting an audience of royalty and celebrities. It packs a lot into its one day in mid-July. The highlight of the morning (it starts at 11 a.m.) is the Diamond Jubilee Trophy, a match that showcases the best of current British talent. The main event of the afternoon is the Coronation Cup, inaugurated in 1911 to celebrate the coronation of George V and still the jewel in the crown of the polo world. There is also a star-studded evening party, seen by many as the highlight of the Season (though the Royal Academy might have something to say about that – see page 74). With celebrity disc jockeys, aerial circus displays and fireworks on offer, there is no denying that the party sponsor – luxury club Chinawhite – pulls out all the stops. You need to belong to Chinawhite, or other designated clubs, or have your name put forward by a committee member, in order to qualify to apply for tickets for this.

'Smart casual' is the official dress code during the day – no jeans, trainers or sportswear, and men are asked to wear collared shirts and jackets when in the restaurant. However, those who have tickets to the evening party will want to raise the glamour stakes considerably.

It is possible to drive to the Guards Polo Club, although private cars require a pass, bought in advance when you buy your tickets. It is also possible to arrive by helicopter – Coworth Park

helipad is five minutes' drive away.
Otherwise, take a train to Egham
or Sunningdale and pick up a taxi.

*Her Ladyship has
always found polo a
baffling sport, rather
like a speeded-up version
of croquet on horseback.*

A bit about polo

Her Ladyship has always found
polo a baffling sport, rather like a
speeded-up version of croquet on horseback (and she doesn't
understand the rules of croquet either). So on the assumption
that some of her readers may be similarly ignorant, she here
offers a brief summary of how it is played.

The game is said to have originated in Persia as much as
2,500 years ago, but the modern form developed in India in the
nineteenth century and was brought to Britain in the 1860s. The
name derives from the word for 'wooden ball used in polo' in a
Tibetan dialect spoken in Kashmir – a dialect known (and this
may surprise many restaurant-goers in the West Midlands) as Balti.

At the top level a game is played between two teams of four
on a ground 275 metres (300 yards) long, with goal posts at each
end. Individual players are given a handicap based on past
performance, so that having the world's best player in your
team may give you a disadvantage of as much as twelve goals.

The handicap system means that there are also three grades
of competition: high, medium and low goal, with high goal being
for the highest ranking players. The terms refer to the number
of goals in the handicap – the goalposts themselves do not move.

Her Ladyship is pausing for a cup of tea here and suggests
that her readers might like to do the same.

The game consists of eight periods called chukkas (from the
Hindi for 'a round'), each seven minutes long. Now here is the
truly confusing bit: in the interests of fairness, teams change ends
not at the end of each chukka, which would be often enough for

most spectators, but whenever a goal is scored. So unless you are *really* paying attention you are never quite sure who is playing in which direction.

At the start of the game, and the start of each chukka, the two teams line up beside one of the umpires (there are two, both on horseback) and the ball is thrown in between them. Then – or so it seems to Her Ladyship – all hell breaks loose as players start swinging their mallets (you see, it *is* croquet on horseback) and trying to smash the ball towards the goal. The various players are designated as attacking or defensive (and Number 3 has been likened to the pivotal position of quarterback in American football), but these definitions are flexible and any player may turn up on any part of the ground at any time. Although there is no concept of offside in polo, there are strict rules about which player has the right of way and how a player may be challenged – as much as anything to make the game as safe as possible for the ponies.

And then, finally, after that hectic seven minutes, a bell goes, play stops for three minutes and the ponies pause for breath – or take the rest of the day off. They are not allowed to compete in more than two chukkas in an afternoon, with a rest of at least one chukka in between. At the top level, players have a pony for every chukka.

Polo is, undeniably, a game of great skill and should not be attempted by anyone who is not already a highly competent horseman/woman. The rule about ponies playing only two chukkas means, also, that every player needs at least four ponies for every match, so it can attract only the very well-heeled. Husband prospects, therefore, are excellent, especially if your taste runs to athletic royalty.

Cowdray Park: polo's other home
Polo's other prestigious venue is Cowdray Park, whose involvement in the game goes back almost as far as Hurlingham's – the first

tournaments were played here in 1910. Polo nearly died out in England during the Second World War and its post-war revival is largely credited to the 3rd Viscount Cowdray. He not only built up a first-rate string of polo ponies, he turned part of Cowdray Estate into an internationally famous polo ground and hosted the first post-war Coronation Cup in 1953. The fact that he had over 6,000 hectares of glorious countryside (now encompassed by the South Downs National Park) at his disposal must have helped to attract the crowds.

Today Cowdray's highlight is an international match, between England and the United States, held on a Saturday in mid-May. This is the first high-goal fixture of the season, so a key event for enthusiasts. From mid-June to mid-July there is the Gold Cup, first competed for at Cowdray in 1956.

Tickets, which are not expensive, are generally available on the day; the exceptions are the semi-final and final of the Gold Cup, when it is prudent to book in advance (from early May). The atmosphere is relaxed, with smart casual clothing (no shorts in the Members' Enclosure is the only specific restriction) and shoes appropriate to the weather.

A word of warning: Cowdray has two sets of 'lawns', about 5km (3 miles) apart; the venue for each event is subject to change and not confirmed till the day before. Keep an eye on the website and make sure you go to the right place. The nearest stations (Haslemere and Pulborough) are 15km (9¼ miles) away, so – much as it pains Her Ladyship to say so – going by car is almost certainly the best plan. The roads round about are some of the prettiest in England, but many of them are windy, single-carriageway and, on polo days, full of horse boxes: allow plenty of time if you don't want to risk missing the opening chukka.

The Open Championship

There are those who call this event the Open Golf Championship – we can forgive them, because they are probably trying to be helpful to outsiders. Those who call it the British Open, on the other hand… Well, to be fair, Her Ladyship must admit that those who call it the British Open are likely to be Americans, and they do have an Open of their own.

The Open takes place over four days, Thursday to Sunday, at the end of the third week in July. It was first played at Prestwick in Scotland in 1860, but is probably unique in terms of the Season's sporting events in that it does not always take place in the same country, never mind on the same course. (Her Ladyship is writing at a time when a campaign for Scottish independence is much in the news, so feels it prudent to underline the difference between England and Scotland, just in case political events overtake her.)

Open venues

There are nine possible venues for the tournament; it tends to be in Scotland one year, England the next, with St Andrew's – as the home of golf – quite rightly having more than a ninth share. The venues are all links courses, which means, for the uninitiated, that they are by the sea and are large, open and undulating. The dress code should thus speak for itself: large umbrellas are not called 'golfing umbrellas' for nothing and those chunky pullovers with the diamond patterns come into their own on a links course.

Those chunky pullovers with the diamond patterns come into their own on a links course.

If you want to go to the Open this year, or indeed every year, of course, you have to go where it's being played. If, on the other hand, you'd like to go once in your lifetime, it might help you make a choice to learn a little about each venue.

St Andrews, Fife: The Royal and Ancient Club at St Andrews is the MCC or Wimbledon of golf – the spiritual and regulatory home of the game. All sorts of traditions can be attributed to it: golf is said to have been played at St Andrews 600 years ago[5]. It was also here that the nineteenth-century golfing authorities decided to make the standard course eighteen holes long.

An important warning about St Andrews: it has a total of seven golf courses (quite a lot for a town of 17,000 people). The Open is played on the Old Course which, despite long and close associations, is not the same thing as the Royal and Ancient Club. Make sure you go to the right place. The other courses are all charming, but won't be what you want if you are celebrity spotting.

Other courses in Scotland...

Carnoustie, Angus: it has been said of Carnoustie that 'When the wind is blowing, it is the toughest golf course in Britain. And when it's not blowing, it's probably still the toughest.' The majority of the Open courses are on the west coast, but the winds here on the east can be particularly challenging to even the best golfers. As a spectator, you have been warned: wrap up well.

Muirfield, East Lothian: regarded as perhaps the fairest test of golfing prowess, for reasons that Her Ladyship finds too technical to go into here. Suffice it to say that if you lose at Muirfield, you can't decently blame it on a bad bounce.

---

[5] The Old Course at Musselburgh, near Edinburgh, is in the *Guinness Book of Records* as the oldest course in the world, with records dating back to 1672 and the rumour that Mary, Queen of Scots, may have played there a century before that. Maybe so, but in 1547 – when Mary, Queen of Scots, was a mere child – golf at St Andrews was popular enough for King James II of Scotland to ban it on the grounds that it was distracting young men from archery practice. Archery isn't a major feature of modern warfare, but at the time it was deemed more useful to the defence of the realm that hitting a ball along a track hacked through the heather.

Royal Troon, Ayrshire: the experts pray that the wind is in the right direction when they play here – playing into the wind on the last few holes is as tough a proposition as any to be met in golf. This makes it another place where spectators are advised to dress to suit the weather.

Turnberry, Ayrshire: the most recently adopted of the Open venues, its first tournament having been held in 1977. It is, however, arguably the best place on the circuit to stay. Turnberry was the world's first golf resort and the attached hotel, recently refurbished at some expense, has suites overlooking the sea, views over the golf course, the opportunity to ride along the beach at sunset – it is a paradise even for those who aren't interested in golf.

…and in England

Royal Birkdale, Southport, Lancashire: one of three great golf courses in the northwest of England, where the sand is clearly of the perfect quality for bunkers. Take the chance to head just a mile or so south to Crosby Beach and admire the eerie cast-iron statues of Anthony Gormley's *Another Place* staring out to sea.

Royal Liverpool, Hoylake, Wirral: not one of the household names of golf, Hoylake has nevertheless been chosen as the venue for 2014. Its great claim to fame is that Bobby Jones won here in 1930, on his way to becoming the only man ever to complete a golfing Grand Slam in a single calendar year. Even those who really don't care about golf are likely to have heard of Tiger Woods: widely considered the best golfer the world has ever seen, he has had four consecutive victories in Grand Slam tournaments, but spread over two years. In terms of Grand Slam statistics, therefore – and golf as a sport is almost as fond of statistics as cricket – American amateur golfer Bobby Jones outranks Tiger Woods, which is no mean achievement. If you happen to be at Hoylake in 2014, you will make your mark on a lot of people who know more about golf than you do by producing this piece of information. Unless, of course, Mr Woods, or anyone else, wins all four Grand Slam tournaments before then – keep your eye on the back pages of *The Times*.

Royal Lytham & St Anne's, Lancashire: not everyone remembers to put in the ampersand, but the club takes its name from what were once two separate villages (they are now officially part of the same conurbation, though most of the residents prefer to ignore this fact). True patriots – of a certain age – will remember that it was here in 1969 that Tony Jacklin became the first Englishman for 15 years to win the Open; others will say that the course's high note came in 1979, when Severiano Ballesteros drove a ball into the car park, hit a brilliant recovery and went on to win the tournament. If you want to talk about golfers having élan, Seve (the golfing world seems always to have been on first-name terms with him) is the man to throw into the conversation.

Royal St George's, Sandwich, Kent: it is foolhardy to be anti-Scottish on a golf course – after all, the Scots invented the game. But if you simply can't resist the temptation, Sandwich is the place to indulge it: this was the first English course to host the Open, in 1894. But be careful – no Englishman has won here since 1938, nor indeed has any Englishman won the Open since 1992. *Sotto voce* and off the record, the English should perhaps admit that it isn't really their game and, if recent results are anything to go by, discover a Northern Irish ancestor or two.

When you get there

Having established which venue you need to go to, as a golfing spectator you have another challenge to face. You can't just sit and watch the game. The usual length of a course is around 7,000 yards – golf has sternly resisted going metric, but that is close to 6.5km. You have a choice, therefore. Option one: buy a ticket that gives you access to the course and then either wander around and follow the play as best you can (some people choose to follow an individual player for the whole day) or find a position that you like and stay there, waiting for the players to come to you. There are free-of-charge, first-come first-served grandstands throughout the course. Alternatively, go for the eighteenth-hole grandstand, with allocated seats, so that you have a – well, a grandstand view of the climax of the day's play. All tickets, particularly the more luxurious options, need to be purchased well in advance.

The Open is a wonderful opportunity for early birds: on the first two days, the first players tee off at 6.30 a.m. Others follow at regular intervals, two at a time, until about 4 p.m. If you're following an individual player, you should be aware that he will take around five hours to complete the course.

A bit of vocabulary

A young lady concentrating on the delights of the Season can hardly be expected to know much about golf, but it is possible that her companions will. Her Ladyship therefore offers a brief rundown of some technical terms.

The idea is to *go round* in the least number of *strokes* (small is beautiful in golf scores). Each of the holes on the course is allocated a *par* – the number of strokes, usually three, four or five, which a good golfer will take to put the ball in the hole. One under par is called a *birdie:* the much rarer two or three under par are an *eagle* and an *albatross* and are cause for celebration.

Each hole begins at the *tee*, which means both the little peg on which the player places the ball and the area around it. He drives the ball, using a club called a *driver* – likely to be a *wood* on a long hole, an *iron* on a short one. A good stroke will land the ball on the *fairway* – the lawn-like bit up the middle. A shot that goes astray may land in the *rough*, or in a *bunker*, one of those sandy holes that look as if they shouldn't be there. A player's second and third shots may be played with an iron; he may then *chip* up on to the *green*. The green is the closely mown area surrounding the hole, which is marked with a *flag* or *pin*. Once on the green he will use a *putter* to *putt* the ball into the hole. He and his playing companion will then move on to the next tee and the whole process begins again.

Learning the words wood, iron and putter will cover you for most conversations concerning golf clubs: throwing in the names of historic clubs such as the mashie niblick may tell the more literate of your companions that you have been reading P G Wodehouse, but it will also show that you know precious little about modern golf.

Another important piece of terminology: the tournament typically starts with about 150 competitors. At the end of two days this number is reduced by about half, so that only the top 70 or so go forward to play in the third and fourth rounds. Those who are eliminated at this stage have *not made the cut*.

The trophy awarded to the winner of the Open each year is the *Claret Jug* – not from its colour but from what you would traditionally have put in it.

Have these facts and figures at your fingertips and there is no reason not to acquit yourself respectably at any golf tournament; you may even strike up a conversation with someone who finds you stimulating.

AN IRISH INTERLUDE

This may astonish those whose memories do not stretch back
to the days of long, hot summers, but London used to be
unpleasantly warm in July. The *haut monde* therefore betook
itself to Dublin for the horse show and a breath of fresh air.
The latter was often to be enjoyed dashing from one drinks
party or ball to another – in a milieu not noted for sobriety,
those few days in Dublin stood out as the occasion when one
Social function really did blur into another.

Although it remains a fixture of the Season, the
Dublin Horse Show is also a place for true horse-lovers.
Masters of Hunts from all over the world come to assess the
horses on display and add to their stock. A highlight of the
week is the competition for the Aga Khan Trophy, donated
in 1926 by the then holder of that title as a prize in an

international show-jumping competition. The first winners were – somewhat surprisingly – the Swiss, though the Irish are proud to assert that they achieved this feat entirely on Irish-bred horses.

Irish hunt balls are still held at around this time of year and still have no reputation for sobriety. In England, hunt balls are held at whatever time of year is convenient to the local hunt: Her Ladyship has come across them as early as February and as late as November, and many throw in a Christmas gathering as well. Although they are still occasions for dressing up, wining, dining and dancing, and raising money for charity, they attract hunting enthusiasts and their friends and relations of all ages. Better to take a partner than to rely on meeting someone eligible.

Eight

AUGUST

On the twelfth of August you will go north to shoot grouse,
on the first of September you will return south to shoot partridge,
on the first of October you will shoot pheasants.

Vita Sackville-West (1892–1962)

Glorious Goodwood

Goodwood is now almost as famous for its 'Festival of Speed' as
it is for its festival of horse racing, but the latter is the traditional
Seasonal attraction and has earned the epithet 'Glorious'. The
Festival of Speed, however, entices 150,000 people and an
impressive array of vintage cars – not to mention cars and drivers
from the Formula 1 circuit – to Sussex for three days in mid-July.
So it is not to be ignored by those who fancy themselves in a
broad-brimmed straw hat held on with a pastel-pink chiffon scarf.
Indeed, the very fact that the Festival has been called – by no less a
publication than Debrett's – 'the Ascot of the motor-racing world'
ensures its place here.

Like many of the events in this book, the Festival of Speed
revels in the setting of a stately home set in beautiful countryside.
Take a picnic on the sumptuous lawns or dine on seafood and
champagne in the on-site restaurant, admire the cars and the
scenery, and raise a glass to the Earl of March, son and heir to

the Duke of Richmond, whose family has owned Goodwood House for centuries; it was he who, in 1993, revived his grandfather's interest in motorsports and reintroduced this event to the Season's calendar.

The first Duke of Richmond was an illegitimate son of Charles II, said to have been conceived while His Majesty was at Newmarket, so the family's association with horses goes back rather further than its enthusiasm for cars. Having gloried in the Festival of Speed, therefore, come back a couple of weeks later and enjoy the last horse-racing event of the true Season.

Back to the horses

The Glorious Goodwood meeting takes place over five days at the end of July and beginning of August; the third day (Thursday) is Ladies' Day, but from the fashion point of view Goodwood is chic from start to finish. Chic without being formal is its proud boast: linen suits and panama hats are the traditional male wear. This is a fashion set in the late nineteenth century by the future King Edward VII, a keen racegoer who often attended Goodwood with his latest mistress in tow. The most famous of these, Lillie Langtry, had a race named after her that is run to this day, though the

glamorous actress has of recent years taken second billing to the race's various sponsors. Nonetheless, look out for an all-fillies stakes on Ladies' Day and you should find the royal courtesan in the small print.

So much for royal gossip. To return to the subject of dress: the grey top hats of Ascot would be almost as out of place at Goodwood as jeans, shorts or fancy dress. None of these is permitted in the Richmond Enclosure, though cravats or even polo-necked sweaters are an acceptable alternative to ties. Ladies are given no specific code, but dresses with modest tops and skirts to the knee or below, accompanied by large though not flamboyant hats are the norm. The Earl of March himself summed up the meeting's attitude best when he said, 'We don't want people turning up dressed for a nightclub.' So tone down the bling and concentrate on the suave. Be aware, also, of the sloping nature of the racecourse – flat shoes are recommended.

And if strawberries are your passion, Glorious Goodwood is an ideal place to indulge yourself. It's a long time till next Wimbledon, after all.

Cowes Week

Her Ladyship prefers to do her seafaring with the stability of an ocean-going liner under her feet, so she is perhaps not the best person to enthuse about the world's greatest sailing regatta. That said, there are many options for watching from the shore and from a helicopter, and she can become genuinely excited about the latter. For little more than the price of a bottle of champagne in a good London hotel, you can spend half an hour circling the island and watching a thousand racing boats going through their paces.

'The island' is, of course, the Isle of Wight and for a week in early August its population is almost doubled, thanks to the arrival of about 8,000 competitors and up to 100,000 spectators. Cowes Week nestles comfortably between Glorious Goodwood and the Glorious Twelfth and, given that staying in London after Goodwood was once simply unheard of, it was very popular with those who needed somewhere stylish to go before heading for Scotland and the shooting.

A bit of history

Like many of the sporting events in the Seasonal calendar, Cowes Regatta is the oldest and most prestigious of its kind in the world. The first racing here took place in 1826, with a single competition involving seven boats. The following year George IV presented the King's Cup, which was competed for annually until 1939. Again, in common with many other events, the regatta did not take place during the Second World War; thereafter the King's Cup was replaced by the Britannia Cup, presented by George VI and still a major part of the competition today. Since 2011 the overall winner has been presented with the rather unimaginatively named

Overall Winner Trophy, but the glory of the victory far
overshadows the dullness of the name. At the time of writing,
the trophy takes the form of a traditional Scottish drinking cup
known as a quaich; Her Ladyship refers anyone wishing to know
how to pronounce this word to the lengthy discussions on the
subject to be found on the Internet.

The racing

As for the sailing itself, there are up to forty races a day with
competitors ranging from amateur to Olympic standard. To watch,
it is possible simply to stand on the shore, the best position being
near the start/finish line at the castle of the Royal Yacht Squadron.
However, this has the disadvantage of being very close to the
cannons that are fired to start the racing and is therefore not
for the easily agitated. One alternative is to buy a ticket for the
Cowes Yacht Haven and take advantage of the live music and
other entertainment that it provides. Another is to take a
'spectator boat' trip, either on a staid but stable sightseeing
vessel or on the exhilarating RIB (Rigid Inflatable Boat), though
the latter is aimed more at the adrenaline-rush seeker than at
those who really want to watch the racing.

The truly adventurous – though preferably those with at least
a little experience of sailing – can volunteer to be part of a crew.
The Crew Forum section of the website has 'crew wanted' and
'crew available' headings and although this sounds, frankly,
remarkably close to Her Ladyship's idea of hell, she is aware
that there will be many who leap at the chance.

Cowes does have a Ladies' Day (on the Tuesday), but this is
very much a celebration of the achievements of women in sailing
and other sports. If your priority is rather to show off your new
dress, seek an invitation to one of the balls, champagne receptions
or dinners that take place at the various Yacht Clubs throughout

the week. At the risk of sounding elitist, in order to achieve such an invitation Her Ladyship suggests you frequent the champagne bar rather than hanging around the beer tent.

Those fortunate enough to be invited to parties on board private boats will also have the opportunity to dress up, though anyone thinking of bringing her own boat to Cowes is strongly advised to organise mooring well in advance – even competitors have to make their own arrangements and berthing is understandably at a premium during the week of the festival (the Cowes Week website gives useful contacts).

One last word on the entertainment: the fireworks on the Friday night – a 150-year-old tradition – are every bit as spectacular as we have all come to expect firework displays to be.

Travel? Getting to many of the events described in this book is better done by public transport, but this is truer of Cowes than of most. Parking in the town is very limited and visitors are advised to leave cars in Southampton (or better still, leave them at home and reach Southampton by train) and from there take a ferry. Ferries from Portsmouth, Southsea or Lymington will take you to other parts of the Isle of Wight, whence buses and taxis are readily available. Alternatively, Cowes offers a heliport for those who have access to a helicopter.

Husband potential? Pretty good, particularly for those who are invited to the right parties or find a place as a member of a crew. There are undeniably a great many fit young men about during Cowes Week.

The Glorious Twelfth

The start of the grouse-shooting season – 12th August – has always been the signal for High Society to head for Scotland, there to attend another hectic round of balls in majestic but draughty castles and rambling, possibly haunted, country homes.

> *Head for Scotland, there to attend another hectic round of balls in majestic but draughty castles and rambling, possibly haunted, country homes.*

Shooting – usually birds, sometimes deer – is the standard way of keeping guests entertained during the long hours between breakfast and tea – and most birds were and are shot on private estates. Indeed, the law states that all game belongs to the owner of the land on which it is found, so the only safe way to shoot is to do it on a private estate with the owner's permission.

The seasons during which each bird may lawfully be shot are rigidly defined. In Scotland, the dates are:

- **grouse and ptarmigan** (the earliest, hence the importance attached to the starting date): 12th August to 10th December
- **partridge:** 1st September to 1st February
- **pheasant:** 1st October to 1st February

Other birds such as snipe and woodcock also have their seasons, but the above are, for most enthusiasts, the principal game birds. Her Ladyship is not a fan of this sport, but she acknowledges the role it plays in the economies of the Scottish countryside. And that is all she is prepared to say on the ethics.

On the etiquette, however, she can be quite forceful, because if you don't abide by the etiquette on a shoot you run a severe risk of being shot. Much of the British Association of Shooting and Conservation's Code of Good Shooting Practice is based on common sense and courtesy, with 'safety first' of paramount importance. 'Inexperienced Guns [that is, the people using the guns] should,' it says, 'improve personal shooting skills through practice on clay targets and must ensure they are accompanied and supervised by a suitably experienced person.'

It is vital, also, to keep dogs under control, not to wander without permission on to land belonging to someone else, not to stray in front of other Guns (or indeed other guns), to ensure that any birds that are shot are picked up and that injured birds are not left to suffer, and to know and recognise the species you are supposed to be shooting and not carelessly to shoot anything else. The birds that are shot, by the way, are always counted in pairs, known as brace. No one would dream of saying that their bag for the day contained fourteen pheasants: it would always be seven brace. Logically enough, therefore, fifteen pheasants would be seven and a half brace. It's a usage that goes back to the sixteenth century, so it would be pointless to quibble with it here.

If you are invited to a private shoot, it is fair to assume that your host and his staff will take care of much of the Code of Practice; the same applies if you book yourself on to a shooting party. And now that owning and running a country estate in Scotland has become for many a prohibitively expensive business, a fair sprinkling of the draughty castles and rambling, possibly haunted, country homes mentioned above have been turned into luxurious but still atmospheric hotels. Commercial organisations that run shoots can, therefore, offer just the sort of accommodation you would have expected had you been invited to a private shooting party in the 1930s, but with considerably more mod cons. Husband potential is good: this is a male-dominated activity and as long as the type of male it attracts doesn't repel you, visiting a shoot could pay excellent dividends.

It also gives you the opportunity to splash out on smart tweeds – tailored jacket or coat; skirt full enough to enable you to stride across the moors in comfort; and the best Dubarry boots. Make your sporting clothes elegant enough and there is no reason why you shouldn't wear them in Knightsbridge. But, in the course of your moor-striding, don't overlook the breathtaking Scottish countryside: Her Ladyship advises inexperienced Guns to take every opportunity to appreciate its beauty without feeling obliged to shoot at anything.

Don't overlook the breathtaking Scottish countryside: Her Ladyship advises inexperienced Guns to take every opportunity to appreciate its beauty without feeling obliged to shoot at anything.

Burghley Horse Trials

If you began the Season at the Badminton Horse Trials, you may like to end it with another four-star three-day event meeting – at Burghley, in the last days of August or beginning of September. These two occasions make up two-thirds of the sport's Grand Slam and if you are really keen you will have nipped over to the States to catch the third, the Rolex Kentucky, before the Season began. The only person ever to have won the Grand Slam is Pippa Funnell in 2003; feminists may like to note that this is a sport in which women can excel, and it is not obligatory for them to be royal.

The first horse inspection at Burghley is on the Wednesday afternoon, with the 'events' taking place, as they do at Badminton, over the next four days, two days being allocated to dressage. As for dress, comfort rather than elegance is recommended: the grounds of Burghley are undulating, to say the least, and impractical footwear could ruin your enjoyment of the day.

For those who are not keen followers of horse trials, Burghley is perhaps the most shopping-orientated of the Season's events. It boasts over 500 outlets, including a Bond Street jeweller, a number of pavilions under the auspices of the Rural Craft Association, a Food Walk and the opportunity to buy a silk-filled duvet.

Burghley House and Stamford

Although the house is closed during the Horse Trials, it is worth
extending your stay in order to visit it and the surrounding area.
The gardens, designed in the eighteenth century by Lancelot
'Capability' Brown, are best seen – by all but the most equestrianly
committed – when there are no horse trials taking place. Unless
an event is in progress the park is open to the public free of
charge every day of the year; the formal gardens only from March
to October and with an admission fee. There is a permanent
exhibition of modern sculptures, a Garden of Surprises featuring
fountains, a water curtain, a so-called Neptune's Grotto and a
longitude dial, all surrounded by rolling parkland embellished
by lime avenues and fallow deer – it is, and Her Ladyship has
no fear of being accused of hyperbole here, a complete delight.

The house is Elizabethan, built for that Queen's Secretary
of State, William Cecil, 1st Baron Burghley, a wily courtier whose
ubiquitous spy network enabled him to bring about the downfall
of Mary, Queen of Scots. To this day the house is administered
by a trust run by Cecil's direct descendants.

Like all Elizabethan houses, Burghley has magnificent state
rooms – in common with many of his contemporaries, poor Cecil
never knew when Her Majesty and her costly entourage were
going to honour him with a visit. It also boasts an impressive
collection of Italian Old Masters, brought back by successive
generations of the family from their Grand Tours of Europe.
The fifth Earl alone acquired the extraordinary number of
350 paintings and must have been grateful for the prudence that
had led him to marry an heiress. In addition to all this, the house
contains some of the most lavish examples of the work of Grinling
Gibbons, so is a place of pilgrimage for those with a penchant for
baroque wood-carving.

Then there is Stamford, the town in South Lincolnshire on the outskirts of which Burghley sits. Sir Walter Scott described it as 'the finest scene between London and Edinburgh' – and that was many years before the BBC chose it as the setting for their 1994 production of *Middlemarch*. With a near-perfectly preserved seventeenth- and eighteenth-century centre and over 600 listed buildings serving a resident population of not much more than 20,000, Stamford should be on the itinerary of anyone who wants to see what a truly beautiful English town looks like.

Her Ladyship realises that very little of this pertains to the Season *per se*, but she feels that both Burghley and Stamford justify the departure from her theme. And, to return to the point, she did buy an exquisite limited-edition Burghley silk scarf last time she was at the horse trials.

Nine

OUT OF SEASON

'My life is very monotonous,' the fox said. 'I hunt chickens; men hunt me. All the chickens are just alike, and all the men are just alike. And, in consequence, I am a little bored'.

Antoine de Saint-Exupéry (1900–44)

Nowadays not everyone has a country home to go to for the autumn and winter months; nor can everyone expect an invitation to sojourn on a yacht moored off Antigua. So those looking to be entertained must find their pleasures away from the traditional Social circuit. Her Ladyship offers these few suggestions...

Edinburgh Festival Fringe

There are numerous festivals in Edinburgh in the course of the summer and early autumn – a film festival, a jazz festival, the international festival (classical music, opera, dance and theatre), a book festival and more – but when most people talk about the 'Edinburgh Festival' they mean this one. The world's largest arts festival, it runs for most of August and boasts tens of thousands of performances in 250 venues across the city: established and aspiring comedians, drama, street music, concerts in the cathedral – there can be few people who would not find something to amuse them. You can stay in or near Edinburgh for several days and gorge yourself on an array of (generally slightly unorthodox) talent, or, if your house party is no more than an hour or two's drive away, you can attend three performances in the course of the day and be home in time to change for dinner. As you wander the streets from venue to venue you will meet an assortment of people from all over the world.

Many of the overseas visitors will be attending – and be baffled by – the Edinburgh Military Tattoo, a spectacle that everyone should see once in their lifetime. 'Spectacle' is the only word for it: six nights a week and twice on Saturdays for over three weeks vast arrays of military bands perform in front of the majestic Edinburgh Castle. Thousands of performers are involved and the evening ends with a floodlit lone piper playing a mournful tune from the ramparts. Despite the fact that guest bands appear from as far afield as New Zealand and Brazil, it is all very Scottish and very magnificent.

Braemar Gathering

If Scottish games, Scottish dancing or brawny Scottish athletes cause your blood to flow a little quicker in your veins, the Braemar Gathering is another perfect excuse to leave the grouse moors behind for a day or two. The Gathering is one of the few Social events that can be put into the diary with absolute confidence from year to year: it is held on the first Saturday of September, from 9.30 a.m. to about 5 p.m.

According to legend, Highland Games in Braemar go back 900 years, to the time of Malcolm Canmore (Gaelic for 'great chief'), the son of Duncan who was murdered by Macbeth. Malcolm summoned the great and the good (or the large and the fit) of his kingdom to Braemar and offered prizes for feats of strength and skill. Specifically, he seems to have been eager to find a runner who could carry messages for him across his hilly realm and accordingly organised a race up nearby Creag Choinnich. The two elder sons of McGregor of Ballochbuie were the favourites to win, but were outstripped – in more ways that one – by their younger brother. Desperate not to be beaten by his junior, the eldest clutched on to the boy's kilt to hold him back; the lad was forced to discard the garment and complete his victory in a state of undress.

Her Ladyship feels obliged to interpose here that these days competitors wear sturdy underwear with the name of their sponsor's product emblazoned on it.

The modern Gathering dates from 1832; Queen Victoria first visited in 1848 and it has been the object of royal patronage and enthusiasm ever since. There are other Highland Games – a larger but less celebrated festival at Dunoon, in Argyllshire, the preceding weekend, the Cowal Gathering, billed as 'the largest in the world' and dating from 1894, and, perhaps inevitably, two vast annual events run by Caledonian Societies in the United States – but Braemar's proximity to Balmoral Castle ensures it its place in the Social Calendar.

The modern games

Although the programme includes Highland dancing, piping, the traditional hill race and the wonderfully named long leap, the true attractions of Braemar are the so-called Heavy Events. These are all about throwing things – hammers, stones and the famous caber – and give every opportunity for spectators to admire the swirling kilts (and sponsored underclothing) of the competitors. No one who has spent a day at a Highland Games

No one who has spent a day at a Highland Games can be in any doubt about whether or not anything is worn under the kilt.

can be in any doubt about whether or not anything is worn under the kilt, though there may be some who are disappointed with the answer.

As may have become clear earlier in the book, Her Ladyship believes firmly that all sporting events become more interesting if you have some understanding of them. She feels, therefore, that a few words about caber-tossing will not go amiss. The intriguing things about it are that there are no rules about the size of the caber, nor does it matter how far it is thrown. The important aspect of tossing a caber – and remember, this is an object resembling a tapered telegraph pole that may be twice the height of the contestant and weigh goodness knows what – is accuracy. It needs to land as nearly as possible directly in front of the thrower: in a straight, 'twelve o'clock' position.

Ladies, the Braemar Gathering may not be the most obvious place for your daughter to look for a husband, but if she chooses a caber-tosser she can rest assured that he is endowed with that all-too-rare masculine quality, subtlety.

The only practical way to reach Braemar is by car: there is a bus service but no railway. The town is 100km (62 miles) west of Aberdeen and about 150km (93 miles) north of Edinburgh, both very scenic drives. In the absence of an invitation to Balmoral, there is plenty of attractive accommodation available, some of it built in the imposing local grey granite, which glistens in rain and sun alike (though perhaps more in rain for the simple reason that it has had so much more practice). Braemar lies within the Cairngorms National Park and the scenery is incomparable.

Dress code: you are in Aberdeenshire. Come prepared. If you are invited to the Royal Pavilion, you will receive more detailed guidance, but even there the Princess Royal has been photographed keeping her ears warm in a hat that she probably would not have worn to Goodwood.

St Leger

For those who want to continue racing after the Season is over, early September offers the St Leger. It is the oldest classic race in the calendar (run for the first time in 1776) and the only one to be held north of the Trent. Her Ladyship knows of no other reason for venturing to Doncaster, though aficionados of the trolley bus may disagree: a museum in its honour – with the world's largest collection – is situated a short way out of town, conveniently in the same direction as the racecourse.

The St Leger is the highlight of a four-day racing festival, which itself is embosomed in a ten-day period of jollification in the town, including champagne breakfasts, live music (from rock to opera) and heritage walks. The usual smart-but-not-formal dress code applies to all but the Grandstand and Family Enclosures on race days: collared shirts for gentlemen, with jacket and tie for the Premier Enclosure; ladies and children to be smartly dressed. The recent refurbishment of the stand has brought an undeniable stylishness to the restaurants and hospitality areas, and Ladies' Day (the Thursday of the festival; the big race is on Saturday) remains an excuse to wear – weather permitting – floating summer dresses and eye-catching hats.

Having written the above, Her Ladyship feels obliged to stop and wonder whether 'eye-catching' is entirely a felicitous adjective to apply to hats. In these health-and-safety-conscious days, she should perhaps point out that she hopes the hat will metaphorically catch someone *else's* eye (through its pleasing design and colour) rather than literally catching the wearer's eye (through, perhaps, an unfortunately placed hat pin).

Last Night of the Proms

Billed as 'the world's greatest classical music festival', Sir Henry Wood's famous Promenade Concerts at the Royal Albert Hall begin in July and continue into September. They therefore provide an excuse to remain in London for the music-lover who has not received an attractive invitation to spend the summer elsewhere; and given that they offer at least one concert a day for almost two months it would be a jaundiced concert-goer indeed who found nothing to please her in the programme. Choral music, chamber music, great symphonies, comedy concerts – all musical notes and harmonies are here.

In addition, the Proms have always had a reputation for introducing new music and talented young musicians and composers: under Henry Wood, who conducted the concerts from their inception in 1895 to his death in 1944, the Proms witnessed the world or British premieres of 716 works by 356 composers. Her Ladyship had no idea that there had been 356 composers in the history of the world (she could probably manage to name 35), so she passes on this statistic with unembarrassed awe.

The concerts are called 'promenade' because those who choose to do so may buy cheap tickets and stand or promenade in the Albert Hall's arena (just in front of the stage) and gallery (way up near the roof). Those who, like Her Ladyship, feel that standing is something one does when the National Anthem is played, and not always then, can pay rather more and have a comfortable seat. But the point of the Proms is and has always been to introduce classical music to a wider public by including 'popular' pieces in the programme and keeping prices low. In the early days you could go for a shilling (5p); nowadays a promenade ticket for a single concert costs £5. Both promenaders and those who prefer to sit may buy various levels of season ticket that reduce the prices for individual concerts still further.

Tickets for the Last Night

A full season ticket also includes admission on the final evening, which is always a Saturday. The Last Night of the Proms is different from all other concerts in the season – probably from all other concerts in the world – and is one of the most British of British institutions. The second half of the programme traditionally includes 'Jerusalem', 'Rule Britannia', 'Land of Hope and Glory' and a medley of sea shanties, with rapturous audience participation and much waving of Union flags. In this multi-cultural age there are those who feel the whole thing is anachronistic and imperialistic, but for the crowds who attend it or watch it on vast screens in parks around the country, it is an annual excuse for loud but generally harmless fun.

Tickets are always very much in demand and may be applied for in one of two ballots from late April. Promenade tickets are offered for sale in stages from July and a few are held back to be sold on the day to those who are willing to queue. Because specific positions in the arena and gallery cannot be reserved, promenaders who hold tickets should go to the Albert Hall on Friday afternoon and add their name to a list, which allocates them a queue number. They should then return to queue in an orderly fashion by 10 a.m. on Saturday, but at least this prevents them having to sleep in the street on Friday night.

Up to 1,400 people promenade at any one concert, in a casual and friendly atmosphere – the dress code is very much 'come as you are' – and there are over seventy concerts in the Proms season. So the chances of a music lover meeting a congenial fellow music lover are excellent. Her Ladyship can vouch for one happy couple who bonded over a shared love of Scriabin, but she hastens to assure her readers that an enthusiasm for Beethoven, Handel's Water Music or even, if the 2012 season is typical, Wallace and Gromit, could serve equally well.

Wexford Festival

Opera lovers who also relish the opportunity to go to a charming Irish seaside town should leave space in their diaries for the Wexford Festival in late October and early November. Founded in 1951 under the auspices of the Scottish novelist Compton Mackenzie, the Festival now boasts its own 770-seater Opera House. It offers three productions a year and prides itself on introducing or re-introducing its audiences to neglected masterpieces. Recent productions include works by Francesco Cilèa, Emmanuel Chabrier and Roman Statkowski, and if you just said, 'Who?', then the organisers would feel they had made their point.

The town is also *en fête* throughout the Festival fortnight; there are daytime concerts, late-night entertainment and, as the website puts it, 'something in the air that quickens everyone's pulse'. Certainly Wexford seems to be addictive: many of Her Ladyship's acquaintance 'get up a party' and go year after year. While evening dress is suggested for the opera itself, daytime events are relaxed and informal, with the opera merely a part of a broader social occasion. Some would say that the Wexford Festival was the embodiment of the well-known Irish maxim that a stranger is a friend – or even a husband – you haven't met yet.

London to Brighton Veteran Car Run

If Goodwood's Festival of Speed has whetted your appetite for stylish old cars, this event will brighten an otherwise dull Sunday in early November.

The most commonly asked question about the Run is why it should take place – in open-topped cars – on a day when the weather is likely to be dreadful and the daylight hours limited. Surely this is precisely the sort of occasion that should be slotted into the spring or summer calendar?

The answer is that it celebrates the date in 1896 when the 'Locomotives on the Highway' Act came into force, the speed limit was raised from 6km (3¾ miles) an hour to just under 23km (14 miles) and it was no longer obligatory to have a man carrying a warning flag walking in front of your vehicle. For motoring enthusiasts this was a tremendous breakthrough and the first London to Brighton Run took place on the day the Act came into force. It didn't happen again until 1927 but since then, apart from

going into abeyance because of the Second World War, it has become an annual event.

Groups of about a dozen cars leave Hyde Park at two-minute intervals in the early morning. The Run – approximately 100km (62 miles) – takes around three to three-and-a-half hours to complete. Much of it goes along the A23, the main London-to-Brighton road, but some follows minor roads where local pubs hold celebratory events. The route is well publicised and there is no problem about taking up a position along it and watching the veteran cars go by. No problem, that is, unless you find yourself stuck behind something pootling along at 30km (18½ miles) an hour. If you prefer to spend the day in Brighton, the official finish is in Preston Park; cars then parade along Madeira Drive.

If you want to enter, you need a car built in 1904 or earlier. Bonhams Auctioneers hold an auction of Veteran Motor Cars and Related Memorabilia on the Friday before the race, so take your chequebook (the vehicles often go for six-figure sums) and see if you can pick up a Cadillac Model A Two-Seater Runabout or a Panhard-Levassor Type A 7hp Twin-cylinder. Fill in an application form online, cross your fingers and hope to join the other 600 vehicles next year. For obvious reasons given the speed the vehicles were built to attain, this is not a race: anyone who reaches Brighton by 4 p.m. earns a medal, but otherwise it is all about the glory and the celebration of this nostalgic form of transport.

Participants are also invited to a celebratory Gala Dinner (black tie, please) at the Brighton Metropole Hotel, where the 33 participants in the 1896 Run toasted that first achievement. It's fun – and likely to have a decent complement of unattached men. Just find (and learn to start) a suitable car...

A word of warning: this is November. That lovely hat and chiffon scarf that were so becoming at Goodwood may not be the most practical of headgear.

Literary Festivals

Attendance at these could occupy the intellectual debutante for the entire year, never mind the Season, but Her Ladyship would draw readers' attention to the words of warning about bluestockings given on page 33. The principal festivals are Oxford (late March), Hay-on-Wye (late May/early June) and Cheltenham (early October), but on a smaller scale they take place across the country, from Budleigh Salterton to Burnham Market and from Althorp to York. The larger ones last up to a fortnight, the smaller only a few days, but all are an opportunity to hear authors talk about their work – and to buy autographed copies of their books.

As the phenomenon of the literary festival has spread, so the definition of 'author' has broadened. Lest anyone be frightened off by the word 'literary', novelists, historians and biographers now share the limelight with television personalities, comedians, political diarists and celebrity chefs.

Arrangements vary – in some places you can stay on site for the entire festival or part of it and have all the talks included in your 'package'; in others you simply buy a ticket to hear an individual speaker. Many festival-goers choose their event because of its location (a medieval hall in rural Devon, perhaps, or a waterside hotel in the Lake District) and return again and again; others turn up to support a local event for a couple of hours on a Saturday afternoon. The scope is – almost literally – endless.

Burns Night

The poet Robert Burns was born on 25 January 1759 and, although his poems in the Scots vernacular are incomprehensible to many south of the border, his birthday is still an excellent excuse for an annual dinner. Caledonian Clubs the world over hold Burns Suppers, as do many Scots, both resident and expatriate, in their own homes. Not to mention those who find it an excuse to end the January detox regime a few days early.

In formal surroundings the haggis (the focal point of the menu) is 'piped in' at the start of the meal – that is, escorted into the room accompanied by the playing of bagpipes. Some will feel that the advantage of celebrating Burns Night in a private house is that you don't have to listen to this cacophony, but Her Ladyship would beseech them, for this one night of the year, not to be such Philistines.

Whatever the venue, Burns' poetic 'Address to a Haggis' traditionally follows its arrival. 'Great chieftain o' the pudden-race,' he calls it; and his gloriously bloodthirsty description is recited as the dish is carved and served.

Two points of important detail here. One, the first syllable of 'pudden', although it does indeed mean 'pudding', rhymes with 'mud'. To give it the English pronunciation, rhyming with 'good', will bring down a welter of Scottish censure on your unsuspecting head. Two, if by any chance you don't know what a haggis is made of, don't ask at this stage of the proceedings. Be grateful for the excellent single malt that is often served as an alternative to wine at Burns Suppers, remember that you have been detoxing for a whole 24 days and keep your misgivings to yourself.

The English often remark (sourly) that there is no such festival to mark Shakespeare's birthday, despite the fact that most people would regard the Bard as a greater poet than the Son of Scotland. Her Ladyship would merely observe that those who choose to eat haggis and drink single malt on 23 April are, as far as she is concerned, at liberty to do so.

Crufts

So the year comes full circle and in March the Season is almost ready to begin again. Dog shows – even the greatest of them – are not by most people's standards Seasonal events at all: Her Ladyship includes Crufts because it is the pre-eminent event of its kind in the world, which gives it something in common with other occasions covered in this book. It is also a good start to the year for those who want to accustom themselves to the noise and the crowds they will have to face in the coming months.

Crufts is held at the National Exhibition Centre in Birmingham over four days (Thursday–Sunday), usually in the second week of March. This is in itself another reason for including it here: it is a convenient distance from Cheltenham and finishes just in time for those interested in both dogs and horses to take in the Gold Cup afterwards.

The uninitiated may not be aware that pedigree dogs are categorised into seven groups. Two of these are on display on each day, with one of the larger groups, the Gundogs, having a day to itself. The days on which each group appears rotate year by year,

so if you are particularly interested in seeing, say, pugs (Toy group), dachshunds (Hounds) or Tibetan spaniels (Utility), check the website for the schedule to make sure you go at the right time.

A general entrance ticket (on sale from September) entitles you to wander round the six halls, watch the judging of the individual breeds and any other competitions such as Flyball or Heelwork to Music that may be on in the various rings; it also gives you access to stalls that sell every imaginable canine accessory, dog-related ornament and item of sensible outdoor clothing. A separate ticket is required to gain entrance to the Arena, where the Best in Show judging takes place on Sunday evening.

Her Ladyship's favourite feature of Crufts is the Discover Dogs area, where anyone who is unsure which dog to buy has the opportunity to talk to enthusiasts about the pros and cons of over 200 breeds, and meet attractive and friendly examples of each. It is an indispensable way to discover the difference between a löwchen and a leonberger before you get one home.[6]

Two important features of Crufts should be noted. One, there can be few places in the world where it matters less what you wear – it's the dogs that are immaculately turned out here; and two, you should be prepared to talk about absolutely nothing but dogs for the entire day. If you thought the equestrians were single-minded…

There can be few places in the world where it matters less what you wear – it's the dogs that are immaculately turned out here.

But, as Her Ladyship's younger friends would say, hey. If you're a dog lover, it's hugely enjoyable. If you're not, turn back to page 42, pick yourself up, dust yourself off and start all over again.

---

[6] About 60kg (132lb) difference, so quite important to know if you were thinking of buying it a bed or a lead.

REFERENCES AND
FURTHER INFORMATION

Dates, dress codes, access arrangements, how to get there,
how and when to buy tickets and a wealth of other practical
information on all the events mentioned in this book are
available from these websites:

Queen Charlotte's and other balls
www.londonseason.net

Point-to-point
www.pointtopoint.co.uk

Cheltenham Festival
www.cheltenham.co.uk/fixtures/the-festival
*For the steam train, see www.classichospitality.co.uk
and www.gwsr.com*

The Boat Race
www.theboatrace.org

The Guineas
www.newmarketracecourses.co.uk

Palace Garden Parties
www.royal.gov.uk

Chester Festival
www.chester-races.co.uk

Badminton Horse Trials
www.badminton-horse.co.uk

Chelsea and other RHS Flower Shows
www.rhs.org.uk

Glyndebourne Festival Opera
glyndebourne.com

Eton: Fourth of June
www.etoncollege.com

Royal Academy Summer Exhibition
www.royalacademy.org.uk

The Derby
www.epsomderby.org

Garsington Opera
www.garsingtonopera.org

West Green Opera
www.westgreenhouse.co.uk

Grange Park Opera
www.grangeparkopera.co.uk

Arena di Verona
www.arena.it

Royal Ascot
www.ascot.co.uk

The (Wimbledon) Championships
www.wimbledon.com

Queen's
www.queensclub.co.uk

Henley Royal Regatta
www.hrr.co.uk

Perth Races
www.perth-races.co.uk

The Lord's Test
www.lords.org

British Grand Prix
www.silverstone.co.uk
To arrive by helicopter, see www.flysilverstone.co.uk

Cartier International Polo
www.guardspoloclub.com
For the party, see www.cartierpolo.php

Cowdray Park
www.cowdraypolo.co.uk

The Open (Golf) Championship
www.theopen.com

Dublin Horse Show
www.dublinhorseshow.com

The Glorious Goodwood
www.goodwood.co.uk

Cowes Week
www.cowesweek.co.uk

The Glorious Twelfth
For a range of shooting events and game shows, see
www.basc.org.uk

Burghley Horse Trials
www.burghley-horse.co.uk
For more about the house and grounds, see www.burghley.co.uk

Edinburgh Festival Fringe
www.edfringe.com

Braemar Gathering
www.braemargathering.org

St Leger
www.doncaster-racecourse.co.uk

Last Night of the Proms
www.bbc.co.uk/proms

Wexford Festival
wexfordopera.com

London to Brighton Veteran Car Run
www.veterancarrun.com

Literary Festivals
oxfordliteraryfestival.org; www.hayfestival.com;
www.cheltenhamfestivals.com/literature
For a list of 150 others, see www.literaryfestivals.co.uk

Burns Night
For a description of a traditional Burns Supper:
www.caledonianclub.com

Crufts
www.crufts.org.uk

BIBLIOGRAPHY

Ashelford, Jane, *The Art of Dress: Clothes and Society 1500–1914* (National Trust, 1996)

Austen, Jane, *Pride and Prejudice* (Wordsworth Editions Ltd, 1992 edition)

de Courcy, Anne, *1939: The Last Season* (Thames & Hudson, 1989)

Freud, Clement, *A Feast of Freud* (Bantam Press, 2009)

Hattersley, Roy, *Borrowed Time: the Story of Britain Between the Wars* (Little, Brown, 2007)

Heyer, Georgette, *Lady of Quality* (Bodley Head, 1972)

Hudson, Christopher & Kirsty, *What Every Woman Should Know: Lifestyle Lessons from the 1930s* (Atlantic, 2008)

Kenward, Betty, *Jennifer's Memoirs* (HarperCollins, 1992)

MacCarthy, Fiona, *Last Curtsey: the End of the Debutantes* (Faber & Faber, 2006)

Priestley, J B, *The Edwardians* (Sphere, 1972)

Pugh, Martin, *We Danced All Night* (Bodley Head, 2008)

Sackville-West, Vita, *The Edwardians* (Virago Modern Classics, 2003 edition)

Whiten, Faith & Geoff, *The Chelsea Flower Show* (Elm Tree Books, 1982)

INDEX

154